The Cooperative Movement of Yemen and Issues of Regional Development

Dr. Muhammad Ahmad Al-Saidi (ed.)

Professors World Peace Academy - Middle East

Copyright © 1992 by the Professors World Peace Academy

The Professors World Peace Academy
G.P.O. Box 1311
New York, New York 10116

Dr. Muhammad Ahmad Al-Saidi, editor

ISBN 0-943852-85-4

Proceedings of a two-day seminar jointly sponsored by the Yemen Economic Society and the Professors World Peace Academy on May 13 and 14, 1985 in Sana'a, the Republic of Yemen, and other selected contributions.

Cover Design and Layout: Fritz Piepenburg
Printing: Al-Mufaddal Offset, Sanaa

Contents

Dr. Muhammad Ahmad Al-Saidi
Introduction 7

Muhammad Anam Ghalib
Welcoming Remarks on behalf of the
Yemen Economic Society 15

Thomas Cromwell
Introducing the
Professors World Peace Academy 19

Dirar Abduldaim
The Cooperative Movement in North Yemen:
Beginnings and Development 22
    First Concepts of the Modern Cooperatives 23
    The Phase of Actual Establishment 24
    The Revolution Takes Priority 25
    The Economic Situation 26
    The Cooperative Associations 26
    The Constitutional System of the LDAs 27
    Sources of Income 28
    The First Conference 28
    Conference of Donor Organizations 30
    The Second General Conference 30
    Results and Resolutions 31
    Specialized Cooperative Societies 32
    The First General Elections of the LDAs 33
    The Fourth Conference 33
    Achievements by the Local Development Associations 35
    General Objectives of the Second Five-Year-Plan (1982-1986) ...36

Eberhard Lutz
The Local Development Associations and their Socio-political Relevance 41
  The Development of the LDAs from 1962-1973 42
  The Founding of CYDA 44
  The Second Conference of CYDA 46
  The Legislative Framework of the LDAs 48
  The First General Elections 51
  The Third CYDA Conference 52

Fritz Piepenburg
The Cooperative Movement of Yemen: Developments after 1985 55
  The Political Setting for the Rise of the Cooperative Movement ... 55
  The Zeal and Enthusiasm of the Early Cooperatives 56
  The Challenges of the late 70ies and early 80ies 57
  Law No.12 of 1985 58
  Law No.27 of 1985 and Subsequent Developments 59
  Cooperatives in the Southern Part 62
  The Situation after National Unification 64

Vivian Craddock Williams
The Non-aligned Economics of East African Villages 68
  Rural Development and Industrialization 69
  The Village as the Key Unit for Development 70
  Government Intervention - Sensible and Sensitive 72

Dr. Muhammad Ahmad Al-Saidi
Determinant of Income Differentials among Tennessee Counties (1960 and 1970) 77
  Theoretical Background and the Model 79
  The Empirical Results 83
  Conclusion 85

Prof. Toshio Toyoda
The Role of Education in Developing Japan 89
Early Beginnings of Education in Japan 90
Education for Industrial Development and its Problems 90
Historical Review of the Spread of Education in Japan 91
The Role of Vocational Education and Training 93
Technological Innovation and Higher Education in Engineering ... 94
Japan's Development and Human Resources 95

Contributors 99

List of Abbreviations 101

Photographic Impressions of the Seminar 102

Summary in Arabic Language

Introduction

by Dr. Muhammad Ahmad Al-Saidi, Editor

A rise in income for merely a certain part of society, a class, or even an entire region, can by no means be considered as development. The process of development, in simple words, can be measured by the degree to which restraints to national economic growth have been removed.

The restraints are all the more profound, since each may become the cause for the rise of another. These interdependent and mutually affecting restraints then form a vicious circle[1]. It indeed appears to me that the largest portion of problems in Third World countries are rooted in the faulty methods employed for the sake of development, and not in the particular characteristics of the developing society. Thus, there is no stigma necessarily attached to developing societies, making it impossible to free themselves from their fetters of backwardness. And proof is given by those developing countries that succeeded in breaking this vicious circle of poverty.

The decrease in the level of real income in the developing world which is ascribed to the decrease of the level of productivity, causes a drop in national savings. This, in turn, will lead to lower levels of investment, followed by a drop in productivity. This is one side of the vicious circle. On the other side of the circle, the low level of productivity inevitably leads to a decrease in real income, causing the demand for goods and services to fall. The willingness to invest diminishes, and with it the amount of capital employed in the sector of production. The last link of this side of the circle is the low level of output by those employed in the sector of production.

And yet, each developing country has within itself the potential to break this vicious circle by applying suitable ways that foster economic growth. A good beginning is to create additional incentives for investment by following a policy of increasing demand.

One of the problems of the developing world is the fact that development efforts tend to be focused on the capital and maybe a few other cities, or concentrate on a certain region. This policy is bound to lead to an economic imbalance, whereby a particular city, region, or even only a small segment of the society living within that region is reaping great benefit, while the remaining country is left without much noticeable progress. The imbalance then brings about a whole range of new development restraints. One of them is the disproportionate demand of imported luxury goods by a small privileged class in the cities or within a certain region, while the demands of the majority of the population remain stagnant. Capital assets are being diverted to the foreign trade sector (profitable imports), instead of pouring them into a wide range of productive sectors satisfying the needs of large parts of the population and serving as a motor for advancing the process of development. The continuation of this process, which should be termed "partial development" or "disfigured development" causes an ever increasing amount of capital to be allocated to foreign trade. Instead of enriching the economy, the nation as a whole will actually become poorer, since most of the aid money, loans, and other government income from taxes and customs will be earmarked for that particularly favored stratum of society. A great deal of public funds are being used to satisfy the rising demand for luxury items that cannot be obtained locally and therefore need to be imported from abroad. Both, the appetite for such consumer goods, and the level of imports will increase with the lapse of time, increasing the need for foreign currency as well. The rising demand in foreign currency will make its value rise steeply. The local currency, on the other hand, is bound to fall to ever lower levels and face complete disintegration.

The rise of the value of foreign currency will have two grave consequences: on the one side, it will lead to a rapid decrease in the real value of local goods and services, if compared in foreign currency terms. On the other side, it becomes difficult to keep up the same level of imports. The developing country caught in such a dilemma is forced to increase the sales of available raw materials, not for increasing the purchase volume of foreign goods, but merely to keep the old level of imports. Once a country has come to this stage, the government is forced by the privileged minority of society to employ all so-called "efforts for national development" to preserve the level of imports. The prime concern of the government centers on how to obtain the necessary foreign currency to keep the level of imports, thus draining the country of its resources, but keeping the government in power, and if only temporarily.

And while attempting to get away from this deadly web, the developing country looks for new ways of gaining foreign currency. More loans are obtained and higher quantities of natural resources and agricultural products are being exported, taking away much needed foodstuff from the poorer segments of society. Valuable job opportunities are destroyed by heavy government interference into the sector of agriculture. Gradually, the country will find itself burdened with ever increasing debts. Poverty and destitution grow side by side with exorbitant private wealth. The rich become richer at the expense of the sustenance of the poor.

This is not where the problem ends. Other negative impacts will be created as well, such as a growing figure of rural emigrants, rapidly increasing the number of urban population and forming "rings of poverty and unemployment" around the cities. The low level of living quality possibly leads to the spread of epidemic diseases, a rise in organized criminal activities, and moral corruption - all unknown to previous generations of city dwellers. The bottom line is the increase of mouths that want to be fed.

Rural areas, on the other side, are losing much of their productive labor power, reducing the population to a society of consumers. The level of poverty and destitution rises along with the feeling of being underprivileged, if compared with the city dwellers. These people then don't realize that emigrating from their miserable existence in the villages will lead them to even greater misery in the poverty belt of the city.

This is the painful reality. However, it is possible to break away from it by applying suitable development strategies. The impact of investments, for example, can be doubled by simply distributing them in a just and reasonable economic way over several areas and regions. Directing a well planned flow of investments into rural areas, where the largest number of people live, will raise the level of rural productivity, will raise the level of real income, which, in turn, will increase the quality and quantity of locally produced goods and services, adding incentives for new investments, etc.[2]

The process of development demands exhausting and continuing efforts on the part of the entire nation, and the employment of all potentials latent within the society. Without the participation and active involvement of all segments of society, the process of real development can never take off. Whether we look at the problem of development from a political or from a social perspective, we will arrive at the same conclusion: real and lasting development can only be achieved by distributing the means for development among all regions in a just and equal way. The same applies for enhancing the process of "civilizing" the entire nation.

Development can only be achieved by way of cooperation and a broad public participation. Without this, no ground can be won in the strife for achieving a high-ranking and blossoming civilization. The speed of development for any civilization is measured by the extent of improving the quality of life spiritually and physically. That improvement should apply to all people, and come as a result of everybody participating in building his home-country. Cooperation has always been the noblest way of communal work since the existence of mankind.

From the earliest forms of human society, to feudalism, tribal affiliations, all the way up to sophisticated capitalist and socialist societies (with the inherent danger of over-emphasizing a centralized or decentralized handling of politics and economics), mankind has always been dependent upon mutual cooperation. It is the nature of life itself with all its challenges and difficulties, that forces man to cooperate with each other.

The organizational structure and scope of activities of cooperative work have changed and developed in history. In modern times, cooperation came to cover a large area of service-related, productive, and consumer-oriented activities, rather than jointly facing natural disasters and calamities. In the developing world, the cooperative approach is of special importance, not only because it mobilizes many hidden reserves of the people for the sake of development, but also as a way of mobilizing the public and giving incentives to the individual by distributing the benefits of development evenly among all regions. Most governments in Third World countries have very limited resources, making it difficult to finance and implement all the projects necessary to keep up the momentum of national development. The government is then tempted to concentrate its efforts and limited resources to a few major cities. Here, cooperatives and cooperative movements can make a big difference.

Yemen has an outstanding history of cooperative work. In fact, cooperation among the people has always been a most important pillar supporting the survival and development of Yemeni society.

With the two Yemeni revolutions on 26th September, 1962, and 14th October, 1963, the scope of cooperation was increased, and a new phase began characterized by more streamlined and better coordinated projects supported by the government. The government provided new incentives to the cooperative movements and helped them in raising their efficiency.

The booklet is an attempt to clarify the importance of inter-regional development and the need to distribute the fruits of this development just and evenly. The just distribution of income in reasonable and acceptable proportions is certainly one of the main goals of development. The book also describes cooperative work as being the tool and method for development, whose benefits are reaped by the

Introduction

people of the far corners of the country, thus preventing the appearance of so-called "poverty pockets", typical for so many developing countries.

Six contributions are combined within this book. Three of them were originally presented as working papers at a seminar entitled "Cooperative Movements - a World Experience" taking place in Sana'a between May 13 and 14, 1985. The seminar was jointly sponsored by the Yemen Economic Society and the Professors World Peace Academy/Middle East Division. The seminar met with great interest on part of concerned government officials and foreign diplomats serving in Sana'a.

For the sake of completing this publication, we saw fit to add three more contributions. Together with the working papers originally submitted during the seminar, they stress the importance of a balanced regional development and the vital role cooperative movements are playing in accomplishing exactly this.

Part I deals with the Cooperative Movement of Yemen, its beginning, development, and current state.

Dirar Abduldaim in the first paper entitled *"The Cooperative Movement of Yemen: Beginnings and Development"* points to the popular origins of the cooperatives in Yemen. He explains that people had to start from absolute zero. Their initial motivation came from their goodwill and a burning zeal for improving their living conditions. Contributions were limited and came either in kind or in cash. But by donating those contributions, people made real sacrifices for the sake of the public good. Abduldaim then explains in detail the process of establishing the Confederation for Local Development Associations (CYDA) and the convention of the first three conferences. The purpose of CYDA was to assist and serve the LDAs by centrally channeling funds and expertise. The whole experiment received great attention from similar organizations in other countries world-wide. "CYDA was often invited to attend international cooperative meetings and conferences and was greatly applauded and praised." Accomplishments by the LDAs even before the establishment of the first 5-year-plan were remarkable. The first 5-year-plan then guaranteed a successful cooperation between the LDAs and the government.

Eberhard Lutz in the second paper, *"The Local Development Associations and their Socio-political Relevance"*, sheds light on developments before 1973 and the institutionalization of the cooperatives between 1973 and 1975. By meticulously studying Yemeni publications published over several years, he came up with valuable insights and realizations. He points out that the dominance of sheikhs and other notables foiled the plans of more progressive LDA members who attempted to keep the LDAs free from traditional elements. But, at the same time, these traditional elements were well respected and received by the people, for whom it was perfectly alright to have their traditional leaders heading the LDAs as well.

Lutz gives a clear analysis of how Ibrahim Muhammad Al-Hamdi (President of North Yemen from 1974 till 1977) tried to use the cooperative movement for consolidating his own power, thereby disregarding and alienating traditional tribal structures, which eventually led to his downfall. Lutz emphasizes the significance of the first general elections of LDA boards in 1975. For the first time in Yemen's history, the entire population was called upon to cast votes, and not just certain segments of society.

Fritz Piepenburg in his contribution *"The Cooperative Movement of Yemen: Developments after 1985"* gives an overview of the development of the Yemeni cooperative movement after the seminar took place in Sana'a in May 1985. The cooperative movement in Yemen basically underwent a process of increased government control, bringing about two opposite effects. Streamlining and coordinating the various activities of the now-called Local Councils for Cooperative Development (LCCD) can certainly be counted among the positive changes. Furthermore, by strictly organizing the LCCDs according to democratic principles, supported by nationwide elections, an important precedent was created for the first free, nationwide parliamentary elections that took place on July 5th, 1985 in the northern part of Yemen. - On the other hand, the government's rising interest in the internal affairs and structures of the Local Councils thwarted a great deal of the zeal and enthusiasm formerly displayed by its members. Initiatives, organization and funding were no longer forthcoming from the people directly concerned, but left to civil servants and government appointed (and paid) administrators. Yet despite these serious setbacks (gnawing at the very foundation of the self-help idea), the LCCDs could still achieve some remarkable results over the last years.

Part II deals with issues of regional development in three very different countries: Tanzania representing Africa and the Third World in general; Tennessee of the United States of America, exemplifying developments in the Western industrialized world; and Japan, as the rising economic giant, forecasting developments and new power structures likely to arise in the 21st century. All three papers point to the importance of education for regional development to take place successfully.

Vivian Craddock Williams is a man with a long-standing work experience in East Africa, notably Tanzania. In his paper entitled *"The Non-aligned Economies of East African Villages"* he states that agricultural potentials in Yemen are not fully tapped: "Over 80% of the people live outside the towns, yet agriculture and rural industries contribute less than 26% of the GDP." The typical East African village, according to Williams, is an isolated settlement, and therefore a kind of natural self-help community. It is an organic entity, grown over centuries, not the produce of a theorist. Yet, at a certain stage government intervention becomes inevitable to increase the national output. He gives credit to East African countries for keeping alive programs of supporting self-help in a pragmatic and non-ideological way. The government does best by supporting self-help organizations, but leaving the freedom of choice up to the villages themselves. The government, according to Williams, should take the road of instilling ambitions for reaching higher levels of development among the villagers, but then leave it up to the villagers to do the actual job. Williams believes that once the cycle of higher output, higher income, and higher consumption level is functioning, the development progress will take off almost automatically.

Dr. Muhammad Ahmad Al-Saidi in his paper *"Determinant of Income Differentials among Tennessee Counties"* analyzes the factors determining the family income in the 95 counties of Tennessee, USA, in 1960 and 1970. He comes to some interesting conclusions. By employing the equation method he finds that the level of education is the prime determinant for the regional inequalities in Tennessee. Other factors are the degree of industrialization, race composition, urbanization, and the rate of growth of employment. The factor of race composition, believed to constitute a major negative correlation, turned out to be far less important than previously thought. This became even clearer, when the same mathematical exercise was employed for 1970.

Prof. Toshio Toyoda in his paper on *"The Role of Education in Developing Japan"* attempts to explain Japan's "economic miracle" in rational terms. He strongly emphasizes the role played by the national industry and education. Japan has a long-standing tradition of education, reaching back to previous centuries. Four years of compulsory education was already a well established practice at the end of the 19th century, with school attendance reaching 96% in 1906. At the same time, vocational education was improved substantially in close coordination with the requirements of the industry. Half of the educational expenses were carried by the local community, notably by the parents. Much attention was given to developing the engineering faculties of the universities in close cooperation with industrial demands and developments. Japanese traditionally live in small houses. But parents were willing to sacrifice even the little space they had to give their children a special area for studies. A survey conducted in 1979 revealed that 76% of primary school pupils had their own study room. This percentage is higher than in other countries, even in the highly developed industrial West.

1   The most ardent supporters of the idea of the vicious circle would argue that the society of any underdeveloped country is subjected to a whole circle of negative factors, all mutually dependent and influencing each other. Therefore such a society is destined to remain at the same low level of development and change is extremely difficult, if not at all impossible.

2   This assumption implies that the income created by the rural areas will be redistributed in a just and thoughtful way, with special consideration for the lower income bracket. The disappearance of a large portion of this income into foreign channels has to be strictly avoided. Instead, resources should be distributed locally, thereby increasing the demand for more goods. Items demanded by the rural population will differ considerably from those demanded by the urban population. People from the countryside, having only a limited budget at their disposal, will look for essential commodities, which to a large extent can be produced locally. This will provide additional incentives for an increase in local production, thereby easing the demand of foreign currency for financing imports.

Welcoming Remarks on behalf of the Yemen Economic Society

by Muhammad Anam Ghalib, President of YES

His Excellency, Dr. Ahmad Al-Asbahi, Minister of Labor and Social Affairs; Muhammad Al-Shuhati, Chairman of the Agricultural and Cooperative Credit Bank; Ahmad Al-Waysi, Deputy Minister of Labor and Social Affairs; Muhammad Al-Saidi, Assistant Undersecretary of Economics; Muhammad Al-Adi, former Minister of Economy and economic advisor to the Prime Minister! Esteemed speakers and friends from the Professors World Peace Academy, distinguished participants!

On behalf of the Yemen Economic Society I would like to welcome you here in Sana'a, capital of Yemen. Some of our guests have come from the other end of the world, such as Professor Toshio Toyoda, who has come all the way from Japan to share with us development experiences of that Far Eastern nation. I would like to extend my special welcoming greetings to him and the other guests who have come from other countries to attend this seminar.

Our topic will be Cooperative Movements, a World Experience. As you know, we here in Yemen have our own peculiar experience of a very efficient and effective self-help movement, and some of our speakers will give an introduction to this experiment. The Yemeni cooperative movement has been instrumental in developing remote rural areas. Now, in 1985, we can safely say that every village in Yemen, and there are several thousands of them, has access to a feeder road, and there is a school within walking distance for school children. Most of the villages have their own supply of electricity. All these achievements go first and foremost on the account of the Yemen cooperative movement, which is an amazing phenomenon, capable of mobilizing the dormant potentials and resources of the people for the sake of their own development.

I also wish to point out to the timeliness of the seminar. Since the passing of Law No.12 last April, the Yemeni cooperatives have been advancing towards a new and better organized, democratic stage. This law is the foundation for nationwide elections of representatives to the various Local Councils for Cooperative Development. These elections will be free, secret and public elections. We are confident that by the enactment of this law the cooperative movement as a whole will reach a new level of performance and service.

Now let me explain a few things about the Yemen Economic Society, which together with the Professors World Peace Academy is sponsoring this event. The Yemen Economic Society was founded in 1982 with the blessings and much encouragement from His Excellency Abdulaziz Abdulghani, Vice President of the Republic. Membership is open to anyone who holds at least a bachelor degree in economics or commerce, or to those who received their bachelor degree in another field, but continued their higher education in areas related to economics or commerce. Our present membership is a very diversified one, including government officials, members of the public and mixed sectors, and private business people.

The purpose of YES is as follows:
- active participation in building and developing the national economy by undertaking research in the fields of development and planning; raising the level of profitability by offering technical advice to the different economic sections of the country; developing the hidden potentials of the country, and promoting their employment for raising the living standard of the Yemeni people in the present and in the future;
- defending the rights and interests of the economists by practicing solidarity among the society's members; deepening the bonds of friendship and cooperation, and elevating the level of skills; development of efficient performance; facilitation of undertaking suitable business, and providing the members with basic guarantees for practicing their profession according to their full rights;
- combining the efforts of economists through their various business establishments to defend the achievements of the September and October

revolutions, strengthening and deepening democratic life and defending the basic rights of the citizen;
- taking responsibility for disseminating knowledge about the economy, as well as facilitating, encouraging and deepening scientific research by forming groups of researchers for the implementation of general and specific economic studies; organizing business and cultural conferences; publication and dissemination of magazines, periodicals and books throughout the libraries; offering training courses within the country and abroad;
- establishing bonds of trust and relations of cooperation between the Society and concerned government offices by disseminating information on all nationwide economic activities; supporting these activities after due consideration from a scientific viewpoint for the sake of improving the general economic situation of the country;
- participation in activities at all levels of the nation's political and economic life, leading to a comprehensive and balanced development and a life of democracy and justice;
- strengthening ties and coordinating efforts with other societies, associations, and unions within the country in order to broaden public participation in defending the achievements of the revolution, and to promote the role of the public in realizing the revolution's national goals;
- strengthening and deepening relations of cooperation and exchange of expertise with other authorities, organizations, societies, and unions on the Arab and international levels in order to promote the goals of the Society.

The Society has been fairly active in its first three years of existence. The list of completed and planned seminars, conferences and training sessions includes topics like: Economics for Journalists and Media People - Economic and Monetary Development in Yemen - Price Stability, a Composition of Local Production and Imports - The Process of Oil Production and its Impact on Arab League Members' Economies. The current topic on Cooperative Movements, a World Experience will without doubt result in another valuable publication on our country's economic affairs.

Let me finally express my thanks on behalf of the Yemen Economic Society and our participants to the Professors World Peace Academy for generously co-sponsoring this event and bringing to Yemen experts on this topic from the far ends of the world. I wish you all to have a most fruitful and meaningful time throughout these following two days. Thank you all for attending.

Introducing the Professors World Peace Academy

by Thomas Cromwell, Secretary General, PWPA Middle East

The Professors World Peace Academy was founded in Korea in the early 1970s to promote good relations between Japan and Korea. The main concept behind the work of the Academy is that academics deserve to play an important role in problem-solving and policy-formation because of their extensive knowledge and ability to analyze current affairs.

In the case of Korea and Japan, long-festering resentments and tensions could not be surmounted by politicians, whereas PWPA proved that on the academic level a large measure of mutual understanding could be achieved.

Today, the activities of PWPA are truly world-wide. The Academy has chapters in countries as diverse as America and the USSR, Yemen and Uganda.

Each national branch of the organization creates its own programs to address the issues of greatest importance in its environment. Thus PWPA Japan, with a membership of over 2000 academics, is studying the future role of Japan in Asia and the world, while PWPA South Africa, which includes representatives of all the races there, is tackling the thorny problem of Apartheid and racism in general.

In the Middle East, PWPA has sought to study issues that are usually considered sensitive but which lie at the heart of problems obstructing development of the region. Recognizing the need for representatives of all nations of the region (regardless of political or ideological differences) to work together to solve shared problems, beginning in 1984 PWPA is planning to sponsor a series of annual regional conferences[1].

The theme of this meeting is "Cooperative Movements: A World Experience". Experts from Africa, the Middle East and Japan will share their knowledge of cooperative movements and other development trends in an effort to put Yemen's experience in an international perspective.

Of particular interest will certainly be the contribution of a distinguished Japanese professor who will attempt an explanation on how Japan managed to pull itself out of a state of under-development to achieve the preeminent place in the world it enjoys today. The implication is that perhaps the Middle East could learn more by looking to East Asia than to its former colonial rulers for guidance in its development.

PWPA will continue to sponsor activities and conferences that promote a cooperative approach to achieving peace and prosperity, founded on democratic principles and human rights, in the Middle East.

---

[1] Until the date of publication of this book, PWPA/Middle East Division has sponsored six regional conferences, covering: trade and peace, cities, education, agriculture, industry and the relationship between culture and conflict. In addition, a number of smaller meetings were sponsored as well, such as a Turkish-Greek dialogue and a study of democracy in Yemen.

PART I:

The Cooperative Movement of Yemen

The Cooperative Movement in North Yemen: Beginnings and Development

by Dirar Abduldaim, General Director of Computing Systems (MoLA)

Since 1973, the Cooperative Movement in Yemen has been a subject of great interest to many Yemeni scholars and researchers.

In the beginning, most of those scholars' writings tried to focus on the positive aspects of the movement, readily applauding its features for the following reasons: first it was a new experiment, which needed encouragement and support. Second, most of those studies were made at the request of the Confederation of Yemeni Development Associations (CYDA) on certain occasions, such as cultural festivities during tree planting seasons, and in the wake of cooperative conferences. Third, the time given for those studies was usually short and limited.

Therefore, these studies did not succeed in theorizing the cooperative movement. In fact, studies made by a few foreign researchers, proved to be of a deeper dimension.

Most studies about cooperative movements in Yemen trace the movement's origin to the late fifties, when a charitable association was established in Hodeidah in 1958. Other scholars introduced their studies by giving a quick overview of the general concept of cooperation and its historical roots in Yemen. Cooperation enabled people to construct the historic Marib Dam and other irrigation systems, and to build the terraced fields on mountain slopes.

No doubt, the spirit of cooperation is rooted deeply in Yemeni society. Cooperation became necessary because of the difficult topography of the country and its strategic geographical location, away from the main commercial roads and the big markets of the Arabian Peninsula. These factors have forced the Yemeni people to depend wholly on agriculture, founded on a cooperative basis.

Yemeni agriculture had witnessed a severe setback resulting from the destruction of the historic Marib Dam, and a great number of the population opted for emigration as an alternative. Yet again, Yemenis expressed their cooperative spirit by establishing new settlements outside their native country, such as the Kinda Emirate in Najd, the Ghassan Emirate in Syria, and the Mandhar Emirate in Iraq.

Of course, it is impossible for today's scholar to connect those ancient aspects of cooperation with the modern cooperative movement. There is no sequence of evolution between the early phases and modern times, and there are no historical documents clarifying the structure of the ancient form of cooperation.

First Concepts of the Modern Cooperatives

The beginning of modern cooperatives is well documented in the valuable study made by Professor S.M. Salem, and published in the Al-Hikmah Al-Yamania magazine. The author, a professor of history at Sana'a University, published articles written before the 1962 September revolution by Yemeni authors about the significance of agriculture in Yemen, and the need for its development and modernization. The articles also dealt with the urgent need for establishing what we may call agricultural associations. The government and rich merchants were called upon to support and back such a project, helping it financially according to a system similar to what is now known as the Agricultural Credit Bank.

This early phase may be considered the beginning of the modern cooperative movement. For the first time, a systematic structure was laid down in the Al-Hikmah magazine:
- The new idea of cooperatives included a proposed organizational plan.
- The idea was well defined by a number of non-governmental associations.
- It included the essential financing instrument by proposing the establishment of an Agricultural Credit Bank, although it did not, in fact, assume this modern name.

- Its goals, functions and fiscal sources were precisely and clearly defined.
- It explained the advantages and benefits of these associations and their possible expansion.

Despite the fact, that the idea was published and disseminated, social and political conditions at that time were not ripe for the actual formation of cooperatives.

The Phase of Actual Establishment

However, these concepts of cooperation did, in fact, set the frame for what would come next.

After the revolution of 1962, the new regime began to pay attention to the cooperative movement, and for the first time, a law was enacted aiming at the establishment of cooperative societies.

In his book entitled "The Beginning", the author A.H. Alwis said: "The first cooperative association or society in the country was that of fishermen on the Red Sea shore, which was inspired by the Islamic system."

Fishermen cooperated in financing and building a new big ship for the use of fishing in deep waters.

Expected income was to be divided as follows:
- a share for repairing the ship and fishing equipments;
- a share to be distributed among the shareholders;
- a share for the workers on the ship;
- a share for "Al Zakat" - an Islamic tax, half of which should be paid to the government, and the second half be distributed to the poor, and victims of calamities among the inhabitants of the village.

The goals and objectives of the society were:
- to protect fishermen from exploitation and monopoly, helping them to improve their living conditions;
- to provide fishermen with equipment for fishing;
- marketing production at adequate prices, guaranteeing benefits for both, consumers and fishermen;
- conducting evening classes for eradicating illiteracy among its members;
- helping members' families and taking care of the education of their children.

The initial success achieved by those societies was limited. All of them eventually ceased to exist, leaving the field for more successful endeavors and attempts.

The principal causes of their failure were the following:
- lack of popular awareness of the functions and achievements of the societies, due to their inability to absorb and back such societies;
- little attention paid to them by the government, which was wholly involved in fighting to protect the Revolution and safeguard the Republic, whose age was only three years;
- shortage of financial resources and failure of members to provide the money necessary for the financial security of any of those societies. It seems that none of those societies had a constitution. There were only certain unwritten rules. Many of the members did not realize the importance of an organizational structure.

The Revolution Takes Priority

Through the years 1966 to 1967, the cooperative idea emerged again, but on a larger and wider scale.

Some clarification of the motives of those latter attempts is needed here. The Revolution of September 1962 had changed not only the political regime, but also the mentality of the citizen. He began to realize that he was living in the twentieth century. By putting an end to geographical and psychological isolation, he became aware of the progress and development in the world around him.

The Revolution exerted all efforts possible to restructure the country from the very basis. The deposed regime did not leave any kind of infrastructure in the fields of education, health, roads, or water supply.

It may be added that the Revolution had faced animosity since the first day of its declaration. It had to fight on all frontiers to ensure and safeguard its continuation and to establish the new republican regime. Nevertheless, constructive efforts were also being exerted.

The Economic Situation

What were the potentials of the national economy to face both political and economic challenges, such as the lack of money, experience and qualified cadres?

Analyzing the components of the national economy, we find that public funds came from only three main sources:
- Al-Zakat (religious tax) which represented 2.5% of the agricultural produce every year;
- other kinds of commercial and real estate taxation;
- limited customs duties.

These limited sources of income were soon consumed and the government had to resort to:
- limiting expenditure as much as possible;
- printing money, which had a very bad effect on the value of the Yemen Rial, and caused a dangerous inflation (this development was halted when Yemen joined the International Monetary Fund);
- resorting to loans;
- applying for financial aid from Arab and foreign countries.

Hence, the economic situation in Yemen began to deteriorate and became worse and worse, especially when farmers began to neglect their fields, joined the armed forces or emigrated in search for an easy livelihood.

Under these conditions, the government could do little and the task of development was left up to the people. People began to understand that the national duty calls upon everyone to participate and take part in supporting the Revolution, creating a new life by all ways and means possible.

The Cooperative Associations

During 1966 and 1967, the idea of closer cooperation with the government emerged. A popular organization was established for the purpose of combining the efforts of the inhabitants of both the rural and urban areas. Cooperative associations were established on the governorate and district levels in Anis and Al-Hujjariyah. This may be considered the third phase after phase two of establishing the first societies in 1964.

These first cooperatives were organized as follows:
- Representatives of the inhabitants of the governorate or district gathered as members of an administrative board and elected a director or president. The number of members was not limited. It could reach 50 and more.
- People called those boards "The Local Development Associations" (LDAs).
- The association then introduced itself to the people. Acceptance by the people was not a problem for legalizing the Local Development Association, because usually the most prominent citizens were already part of the association.
- Then the government was notified, but it had no right to send any representative to supervise the elections. This situation continued until the establishment of the Authority of Social Affairs in 1968 which, two years later, began to supervise the elections of the cooperatives.

The Constitutional System of the Local Development Associations

Up to 1974, there was no integrated constitutional system to organize cooperative activities, and to identify and define their functions and goals. The Authority of Social Affairs asked every Local Development Association to prepare its own appropriate constitution and to provide it with a copy in order to grant it a working licence. The Authority studied and commented on each proposal. It was then handed to a lawyer who formulated a constitutional system according to legal principles. As a matter of fact, not much of the constitutional system was practically implemented and applied, except in case of urgent need or conflict. But that does not mean a rejection of the system by the LDAs. Work was planned and carried out according to practical needs and necessities without being subject to written rules and regulations.

The Yemeni Cooperative Movement was famous for its large scale of activities and services. It participated in building roads, schools, clinics, water supply systems, and power net works. Priorities were set according to the needs of the population in the area, the nature of the country, and specific conditions.

This comprehensive approach was taken in view of the deplorable condition of the country. Specialized organizations with defined objectives could not satisfy the needs of the Yemeni people who were in need of almost everything. The main question was: "Where should we begin?"

Sources of Income

Before the decision by the government to support the cooperatives, resources were scanty and limited. Only few of the cooperatives had sufficient funds. The majority, especially in the rural areas, were very poor. In larger cities, cooperatives could obtain financial resources. In villages, they completely depended on contributions and donations in money and kind of the inhabitants, which did not help much in realizing their objectives and implementing their plans and projects, even if small and limited in number.

Sources of income of the cooperatives were as follows:
- a certain percentage levied on airline tickets and cinema tickets;
- taxes on trucks and taxies;
- a certain percentage of customs duties;
- financial aid and support by the government for some specific projects and assistance by foreign donors.

People's contributions to the cooperatives were made voluntarily. Official contributions at that time were not decided by the government, but by the administrative boards of the LDAs alone. It is an expression of the spirit of cooperation and self-help, which lies at the heart of the cooperative movements in Yemen.

When the LDAs gained strength and increased their efficiency, the Yemeni people became eager to establish new ones in their own villages and took great interest in their activities. Thus, the years between 1967 and 1978 witnessed a rapid increase in the number of cooperatives in the various districts and governorates.

The establishment of the Confederation of Yemeni Development Associations (CYDA) on June 25, 1973 was considered the beginning of a new and prosperous stage in the history of the cooperative movement in Yemen.

The first general assembly was held upon the request of some prominent members of the 28 LDAs existing at that time. A preparatory committee was formed inviting members of the various cooperatives to attend the conference as representatives for the general assembly. One of the participants of the conference was Abdullah Al-Halaly, who was later elected Secretary General of CYDA.

The First Conference

During the first conference, the name of the cooperative organization was changed from "Popular Cooperative Confederation" to "Development Confederation" in order to emphasize general developmental functions and to be in line with the names of similar agencies world-wide. But soon the administrative board realized that it was wrong to delete the popular cooperative aspect from its name. The conference was renamed again in the second meeting and it became "The Confederation of Yemeni Development Associations" (CYDA).

The first conference elaborated the constitutional system of CYDA, which then became the overall frame, applicable to all cooperative organizations.

The creation of CYDA was a necessity, providing a great impetus to the cooperative movement. It accelerated its activities and achievements and secured such important results as the following:
- demonstrating the unique character of the cooperative experiment in Yemen;
- gathering all cooperative organizations under one umbrella organization, helping to plan their activities and aiding them financially and technically;
- CYDA obtained governmental permission to receive 25% of the Zakat and another 25% of municipal income. Thus, durable and permanent financial sources were established for the benefit of all cooperatives, enabling them to function properly;
- organizing the influx of foreign aid and assistance through CYDA which distributed the funds among all LDAs on the basis of equality, need and economic feasibility;
- CYDA took effective action in coordinating the efforts of the cooperative movement and efforts by the government. Relations between the government and international agencies were formed and coordination between the LDAs and the concerned ministries was achieved for the purpose of implementing certain strategic projects.

Later, specialized departments were formed within CYDA:
- a planning department for studying the plans prepared and presented by the LDAs, providing them with the necessary technical assistance;
- a coordinating department for developing and unifying the organizational aspects and for coordinating with the Ministry of Social Affairs, supervising the elections of the Local Development Associations and solving their problems;
- an international relations department for developing and coordinating CYDA's relations with foreign agencies, cooperative movements and donors, being also responsible for translations and correspondence;
- a cultural and information department for publishing news and the achievements secured by the cooperative movement through the mass media,

gathering studies and researches about cooperative projects and organizing seminars, symposiums, and cultural weeks.

The achievements of the cooperative movement encouraged competition between villages and districts and led to the establishment of more LDAs.

Conference of Donor Organizations

A conference of 12 foreign donor organizations working in Yemen was held in Sana'a from December 12 to 14, 1973 on the initiation of the Central Planning Organization (CPO). The main objectives of the conference were:
- to determine and identify the areas of development requiring help from those organizations;
- to enact the rules and regulations of coordination between foreign organizations and the LDAs through CYDA;
- to determine priorities in project implementation in consultation with the government, the LDAs, and donor organizations.

Aiming at the expansion of the activities of donor and volunteer organizations in Yemen for the benefit of the majority of the population in all parts of the country, the representatives of the donor and volunteer organizations were informed about CYDA's point of view concerning urgent projects in areas of:
- supplying drinking water;
- constructing health centers and building up medical services;
- constructing access roads;
- improving sanitation and social care.

All participants expressed their approval and willingness to support projects apt to meet those needs. The conference finally recommended the establishment of a consultative committee in support of CYDA.

The Second General Conference

On November 10, 1974, the second general conference was held in Sana'a and was attended by the representatives of 65 LDAs. Among the many proposals and

projects submitted to the conference, aiming at evaluating and promoting the cooperative performance, the following were of special significance:
1. Proposals related to the reorganization of the LDAs, such as
   - limiting the number of members in the general assembly of each LDA;
   - opening an account for each LDA in the Yemen Bank for Reconstruction and Development, and submitting these accounts to the Auditing Department;
   - preparing an annual budget for each LDA;
   - preparing an annual plan of projects for each LDA, later amended to preparing a three-year-plan;
   - opening offices with full time workers for each LDA at their location of work.
2. Approval of the afforestation project in all parts of Yemen within three years, aiming at planting three million trees in the first stage.
3. A decision to hold the annual conferences in the capitals of the governorates, taking the opportunity to inform the inhabitants of those areas about the functioning, activities, and achievements of the cooperative movement.
4. A decision to hold the general conferences once every three years, instead of once a year, in coordination with the electoral periods.

Results and Resolutions

Even before the second conference, the government had decided to add another 25% of the income through Zakat to the share given to the cooperatives, making it a total of 50%. The second conference also decided to abolish any kind of tax or customs duty imposed on imported equipments, such as tractors, drills, and generators.

The conference issued some very important resolutions, including the following:
- urging the Ministry of Social Affairs and CYDA to draft a constitutional system for CYDA;
- changing the electoral period of the administrative boards of the LDAs and CYDA from one year to three years;
- establishing an accounting department within CYDA to cooperate with the Ministry of Social Affairs in organizing and auditing the accounts of the LDAs;
- unifying taxes and income of the LDAs;

- calling upon every LDA to prepare a three-year-plan and submit it to CYDA and to the Ministry of Social Affairs.

The conference likewise approved the participation of the LDAs with the CPO in the implementation of the population census.

Because of these recommendations, the second conference may be considered the start of a new organizational stage. Many new systems and regulations were established in cooperation with the Ministry of Social Affairs, such as:
- the amendment of Law No.35 of 1975 according to the experience of the LDAs;
- a unified accounting system;
- the establishment of coordination councils;
- the establishment of 'Uzlas and village systems.

This organizational stage ended in 1976, when a new era, the era of specialized cooperative societies, began.

Specialized Cooperative Societies

After convening the third conference in Taiz in August 1975, which was attended by representatives of 117 LDAs, the cooperative movement began to study the idea of establishing specialized cooperative societies in coordination with the ministries and the authorities concerned. Some agricultural societies were founded and secured relative successes, indicating a bright future for this type of cooperatives.

In February 1978, CYDA organized two conferences for agricultural and housing cooperative societies in Sana'a. The first conference was attended by representatives of twelve agricultural societies. The second was a meeting of urban cooperatives, held for the purpose of studying possible solutions to the housing crisis through the housing cooperatives.

These two conferences did not result in or lead to concrete achievements, except approving a constitutional system for the urban cooperations. Nevertheless, the conferences can be considered a step towards the establishment of specialized societies.

The First General Elections of the LDAs

The elections of 1975 are considered the first of their kind for several reasons:
- proper identification of the cooperatives' general assemblies was achieved;
- election timing at the level of the LDAs was unified;
- a system of direct supervision over those elections was devised, although it was not central or precise.

By then, the cooperative movement in Yemen was able to occupy its proper place on the Arab and international levels. Foreign and Arab experts considered the Yemeni experiment a real success, adding to experiences from countries throughout the world both theoretically and practically.

CYDA was often invited to attend international cooperative meetings and conferences and was greatly applauded and praised. It became a member of the Arab Confederation of Cooperative and Agricultural Societies.

CYDA became the subject of many academic studies, which drew the attention of the international cooperative movement. Among those academic studies was an important one made by researchers of the Bochum University in West Germany. Several Yemeni scholars and researchers conducted these studies, which were then published in Yemeni and Arabic periodicals and in the form of books and pamphlets.

It was natural that negative developments should occur as well during that early phase due to a lack of experience, such as the delay of elections from August to November 1978.

The election period lasted for 70 days, from November 15, 1978 to January 24, 1979 and marked the beginning of a new era for the cooperative movement.

The organization of the election was excellent, taking into consideration mistakes made in the past. It mobilized all material and technical potentials needed to realize the desired success.

As a result, new Local Development Associations were established. Others were divided, reorganized and made functional after having been out of function for some time.

The Fourth Conference

The 4th conference, held from January 22-24, 1979, was the climax of that new era because of its large representation. It was attended by thirty delegations from

Arab and foreign countries, besides the large number of members and participants representing 173 LDAs.

The preparatory committee submitted several studies to the conference. Among them was a project for a constitutional system for a Cooperative Bank. The Bank should have YR 100 million as capital, 60 million of which was to be provided by the Yemeni government.

Other constitutional systems were submitted for agricultural and vocational cooperatives and for CYDA itself.

The basic characteristics of this new era were:
- emphasis on cooperative legislation being expanded in the new draft laws;
- shaping the project of a Bank of Cooperative Development as a new element supporting and backing the cooperative movement, and especially assisting projects suffering from financial shortages;
- promoting the concept of specialized cooperatives to overcome development constraints by establishing a new department in CYDA, staffed with experts for the purpose of organizing these cooperatives. By that time, CYDA had signed agreements with some foreign countries and international agencies, stipulating the provision of training, experts, and equipment needed to promote such cooperatives;
- prompting the Yemeni government to double its financial and technical support to the cooperative movement through CYDA;
- the CYDA constitution submitted to the 4th conference nominated the following officials as members of the administrative board:

    the deputy minister of education
    the deputy minister of information and culture
    the deputy minister of finance
    the deputy minister of public works
    the deputy minister of municipalities
    the deputy minister of health
    the deputy minister of agriculture
    the head of the Social Affairs Authority
    the director of the Bank of Cooperative Development
    the secretary general of the Confederation of Yemeni Emigrants
    the deputy chairman of the CPO
    the head of the Electricity Corporation

These appointments created a direct link between CYDA and the authorities concerned for coordinating their efforts in support of the cooperative movements and to resolve their problems. They were also aimed at avoiding the doubling of activities which happened previously because of lack of coordination.

A new method of planning was approved and adopted. CYDA would now send experts to every village to help the LDAs in preparing their three-year-plans on a scientific basis. These plans were then discussed by the general assembly of each LDA, by the coordinating council, and finally by the department of planning of CYDA to ensure high quality planning according to the needs and priorities of the country.

Achievements by the Local Development Associations

Between 1973 and 1978, the cooperative movement secured many important achievements, such as:
- 13,780 kilometers of road construction
- 2,286 educational projects
- 1,545 water supply systems
- 79 health care projects
- 248 other projects (parks, power supplies, nurseries)

During the early 1980s, the self-help movement acquired new vigor and vision with the establishment of the specialized development associations. Even the service-oriented LDAs achieved great successes.

Cooperative work in YAR was based on popular and collective contributions for providing villages in the rural areas with the basic services which individual efforts failed to accomplish.

The first phase focused on basic projects, such as schools, clinics, water supply projects, etc. The decisive factor for the popularity of the cooperative movement was the democratic process in realizing these projects. People understood that this experiment was their own, and they were not only willing to support it, but to contribute to it as well.

Colonel Ali Abdullah Saleh, President of the Republic, Commander of the Armed Forces, and Chairman of CYDA, gave his full support to this experiment by providing it with opportunities to perform its duties, and by protecting it from direct or indirect manipulation and interference by government agencies. A great number of projects have thus been accomplished during the First Five-Year-Plan:

Cooperative Accomplishments during the First Five-Year-Plan (1977-1981)

Projects	Accomplished		Cost (YR)
Road construction	19,505	km	810,085,227
Road maintenance	6,000	km	48,000,000
Educational projects	4,800	class rooms	244,934,798
Health projects	111	projects	22,278,887
Water projects	1,713	projects	154,662,953
Misc. projects	343	projects	71,182

Since the cooperative movement permeated all areas of Yemen, and only honest elements of society have been selected to perform the work, the political leadership endowed the cooperatives with the task of conducting a popular census.

This census took place over a period of six months in 1981 with the participation of some 4000 helpers and supervisors, most of them from the LDAs. 200 vehicles were used, travelling a distance of more than 13,500 km on roads already constructed by the cooperatives all over Yemen. The whole census, in all of its phases, relied entirely on Yemeni expertise.

Despite the achievements made by the cooperative movement, various problems continued to obstruct its path, particularly in the field of productive cooperatives. Some of the major problems were:
- non-availability of trained technicians;
- increasing prices of machines, and difficulties in obtaining spare parts and maintenance of equipments;
- lack of marketing institutions for agricultural products;
- lack of coordination between concerned ministries and cooperatives;
- widely spread illiteracy in rural areas.

General Objectives of the Second Five-Year-Plan (1982-1986)

The purpose of the cooperative work plan was to assist the government to create quick economic and social development, focussing on the people in the rural, densely populated areas. To ensure fair and equal distribution of services to rural and urban areas alike, the plan focused on:

- providing potable water for different areas in the country, especially for the rural areas;
- spreading education throughout Yemen by establishing schools;
- constructing roads in rural areas and maintaining them;
- providing Primary Health Services for rural areas;
- conducting afforestation campaigns;
- establishing and supporting agricultural and professional associations in cooperation with government agencies;
- completing the organizational structure of CYDA and conducting training courses for its staff.

To implement the plan, the following strategic objectives were deemed necessary:
- coordination with government agencies, particularly technical ministries;
- mobilizing people's capabilities to make donations for the construction of vital projects;
- organizing the cooperative work to obtain the best possible results with the least input;
- spreading cooperative education.

The following goals were specified in the Second Five-Year-Plan:
- to establish three workshops for the maintenance of equipment and machines of CYDA;
- to establish a cooperative institute;
- to launch a project for the maintenance of rural roads (totalling 4,620 km);
- to contribute to the tanning factory project;
- to contribute to the establishment of four marketing centers for agricultural products;
- to establish four plant nurseries for the production of fruit trees;
- to establish a vocational training project for about 5,800 trainees;
- to establish 50-70 agricultural, professional, and marketing associations;
- to contribute to the purchase of 22 mobile health units;
- to participate in the illiteracy campaign;
- to help completing the ceramics factory.

In addition to other projects, the cost of these projects was estimated at YR 614,356,000 ($ 134,432,385, at an exchange rate of $ 1 = YR 4.57).

The more specific goals of the Second Five-Year-Plan were:
- the construction of a total of 3,693 km of roads;

- maintenance of a total of 13,520 km of roads;
- the establishment of 4,513 class rooms;
- implementing a plan to encourage rural students to continue their education;
- the establishment of 812 health units;
- actively encouraging physicians, health officers, and students of public health institutes to spread health education;
- the establishment of 1,206 water projects in rural areas;
- the establishment and support of sport and cultural clubs, mosques, etc.

The total cost of these projects was estimated at about YR 999,385,780 ($ 218,683,971).

Three major plans were drafted for CYDA, the LDAs, and related ministries. The plan for the Confederation and its subordinate institutions dealt with developing the Confederation's capabilities in order to expand and improve its services to the LDAs' organs. This included training, technical, and managerial assistance.

Plans for the LDAs aimed at having them depend on their own capabilities and resources for meeting basic requirements at the village level. Consultations aimed at avoiding miscalculations which frequently resulted from the gap between ambitions/desires and available resources.

The subsidiary central plan formulated ways of coordination with related ministries to satisfy the requirements of LDA projects.

In formulating the projects of the Second Five-Year-Plan, CYDA has considered the following restraints, which became obvious during the implementation of earlier planning:
- the need to conduct a general survey of the work sites and to specify the projects of highest priority by considering such criteria as:
    - density of population,
    - necessity,
    - local participation, and
    - economic and social benefits gained by the project;
- the need to upgrade the level of performance of the LDAs, allowing them to play a more effective role in the nation's economic development;
- LDAs should give priority to vital projects such as roads, schools, water and health facilities. Other projects should not affect projects of higher priority;
- projects of the Second Five-Year-Plan should be planned annually according to their expected revenues for each association.

Beginnings and Development

From this description of the beginning and the various phases of development of the Yemeni cooperative movement, one can only conclude that it is indeed a very successful experiment. It is an experiment initiated by the villages themselves and the villagers were the ones who made it successful. The government came in later and provided a much needed nation-wide service in terms of coordination and central support. Let us hope the movement will continue with the same vigor and enthusiasm it displayed in the early years, and help realize the people's basic needs for years and even decades to come.

The Local Development Associations and their Socio-political Relevance

by Eberhart Lutz, Arabist and Sociologist

When a group of officers proclaimed the revolution on 26th September, 1962, Yemen completely lacked any of the achievements of the 20th century. The ensuing civil war absorbed the energies of the many well-intentioned revolutionaries for many years, and they could not therefore contribute much to the rapidly increasing demands of the people. The question arises of what instrument the Yemeni society could possibly develop in such a situation to solve its complex problems. How did this society meet the big challenge after September 26, 1962? A society which had remained untouched by foreign influences for decades because of the political isolation enforced by its rulers. The Yemenis searched for and found their own way. They formed local self-help institutions which, after a short time, became a well-known concept throughout the country under the name "Movement of the Cooperatives" (al-haraka at-ta'awuniya).

This paper focuses on the institutionalization of the cooperatives from 1973-1975. It attempts to highlight the circumstances which led to the rise of the cooperatives as an independent social and political force.

The Development of the Local Development Associations (LDAs) from 1962-1973

Soon after the revolution, people got together to form associations which were either called "Welfare Association" (jam'iya khairiya), "Civil Cooperative" (ta'awun ahli) or "Development Organization" (hai'at tatwir). The founding of these associations took place spontaneously in the various regions of the country. They aimed at simple infra-structural improvements like the construction of feeder roads, the improvment of water supply, as well as the construction of schools and hospitals on a local level. All projects were financed through voluntary contributions by the people themselves.[1]

The government, most probably influenced by the Egyptian example, paid considerable attention to these associations from the beginning. They were regarded as adequate instruments for the development of the country during a period in which the government itself, due to its political and economic situation, was hardly in a position to contribute much to the construction of the country.

These associations received their legislative recognition through Law No. 11 which came into force on July 3rd, 1963.[2] The law regulates, in 50 articles, the procedure of establishing the associations, outlining their organizational structure, as well as the responsibilities and rights of its members. The government's intention was to create the legal prerequisites for the establishment of any type of association which could contribute to the development of the country.[3] In this way, it legitimized retroactively a citizens' initiative which, by virtue of coming into existence, forced the government to act.

Between 1963 and 1965, eight agricultural cooperatives were formed in the Taiz region on the basis of acquiring shares. They were initiated and supported by the Ministry of Agriculture and its Egyptian advisers. The discontinuation of supportive measures, however, simultaneously meant the breakdown of these cooperatives.[4] While these cooperatives, whose principles apparently were neither understood nor accepted by the people, vanished, the idea of these above mentioned associations survived and developed further.

A first qualitative development of the people's cooperatives (later to be known as LDAs) can be recorded from 1964 onwards. Starting from Taiz, people's cooperatives were founded which went beyond fundraising campaigns. Steady sources of revenue were secured by levying taxes on cinema tickets, fuel, electricity bills and so forth.[5] Although these revenues could hardly have been sufficient to finance the cooperatives' ambitious ventures, it is remarkable that in 1971, these same sources of income were officially conferred to the people's cooperatives by a government resolution.[6] Again it is obvious, that the people's cooperatives challenged the administrative organs to develop themselves in order to keep pace with the people's initiatives.[7]

Beginning from 1968, the cooperative movement suffered setbacks from which it recovered only in the early seventies. The embezzlement of money, as well as the power struggle between the sheikhs and self-conscious groups of young intellectuals caused a part of the population to turn away from the cooperatives in disappointment.[8] It is likely that these internal problems of the cooperatives represented only one of many reasons for their weakness. Another reason was closely linked with the internal political developments, and the political demands made by some of the cooperatives who wanted to limit the powers of the sheikhs and big land owners. One of their fundamental demands was that the state should provide judiciary services free of charge.[9] These demands conflicted considerably with the privileges of the tribal and religious leaders who resolved lawsuits for handsome rewards.

When the royalists' siege of Sana'a had ended in 1968, the republican front was split into two factions: "The republican tribalists led by Al Amri and the sheikhs, and the anti-capitalist left based on the old MAN (Movement of Arab Nationalists) in North Yemen".[10] It is well known that Al Amri succeeded against his adversaries by purging the leftists from the army and the political scene. The political claims were dismissed along with the defeat of their proponents within the cooperatives. This attempt of non-tribal and non-religious elements to set foot in the political scene by using the cooperatives failed.

During the following years, the cooperatives were stagnating and only in 1970 new establishments were reported. This time however, sheikhs and other influential personalities managed to place themselves at the top of the cooperatives. In the founding agreement of the Al Hujjariyah cooperative it reads, "...we are gathered, the sheikhs from Ash Shama'itayn, Al Mawasit and Al Muqatira and notables (a'yan)..., and conclude the founding of the development organization of Al Hujjariyah."[11] The dominance by the sheikhs and notables in the first elected administrative council of 1972 was overwhelming.[12] The names of the representatives from the cooperatives which founded the Confederation of Yemeni Development Associations (CYDA) in 1973, showed that the example of Al Hujjariyah was not an isolated case. With only one exception, all came from well-known families of tribal or religious leadership.[13] The dominant roles of the sheikhs, however, does not necessarily imply that cooperatives do not have the support of the population at large. To the contrary, it is quite normal for the large part of the population to see their traditional leader also as the head of the cooperative. The sheikhs had valuable contacts in Sana'a and abroad. They were expected to be able to mobilize external assistance, which, in turn, secured their positions.

The scope and the organization of the cooperatives in 1970 was almost identical with those of the first cooperatives, founded immediately after the revolution. On a district level (qada or nahiya), they implemented infra-structural measures, whereby the improvement of the water supply was their first priority. Anyone who paid the rather symbolic membership fee could become a member of a cooperative. From the members' ranks, an administrative council consisting of 5-9 members was elected. These, in turn, elected the presidency, made up of the president, the secretary general, and an accountant. For the execution of projects further revenues were collected. For bigger ventures, support was requested from the government or from foreign organizations. In this context, the good connections of the sheikhs to the respective authorities played an important role.

The cooperatives hardly played a role politically between 1970 and 1973. In addition, there were charges of corruption and socio-political confrontations within the cooperatives. Art.37 of the constitution of 1970 forbade the founding of any political party, with the exception of trade unions and associations (Art.38). The cooperative was one of the two legal forms of popular organization in which people committed to politics could be active.

1973 witnessed the establishment of 40 cooperatives, which became active almost exclusively around Sana'a and in the southern regions of Yemen. Until 1972, influence and support by the central government was confined basically to the legislative recognition and the formal support of the cooperatives.[14] The "Office for Social Affairs and Labor", established as early as 1968, and formally responsible for the cooperatives, could not fulfill its role properly due to political and organizational weaknesses.[15] The government, however, soon recognized the political and economic importance of the cooperatives which, on a local level, played a significant role in promoting development in the country. In a socio-political climate characterized by a rather weak central government and traditional mistrust of the tribes, the government had to depend on the local and practically independent initiatives. The cooperatives could then become a potential counter-weight to the traditional powers of the tribal leaders. It was Muhammad Ibrahim Al Hamdi, who not only clearly saw this potential, but also acted accordingly.

The Founding of the Confederation of Yemeni Development Associations (CYDA)

Upon the initiative of Al Hamdi, at that time president of the cooperative of Thula, Deputy Prime Minister, Deputy Commander of the Armed Forces, the representatives of 13 cooperatives including one representative each from the

"Office for Social Affairs and Labor" and the "Central Planning Organization" gathered on March 24, 1973.[16] The purpose of the gathering was the founding of an umbrella organization which should embrace all the cooperatives as well as coordinate their work. Its foremost task was formulated as the "unification of the efforts of the development of the rural society (...) as well as raising the economic, hygienic, cultural and agricultural standards."[17] At the same time, a commission was formed under the chairmanship of Al Hamdi, which was to elaborate a charter for CYDA, and prepare for its first conference.[18]

If one examines the names of the 23 founder members[19] (a few of the 13 LDAs sent more than one representative), all the other founder members besides the two government representatives came from well-known families of the tribal and religious leadership. In addition, all LDA participants with the exception of two came from areas near the capital or from southern regions. One of the two exceptions, the LDA from Khamir, is noticeable for this reason because Khamir is the ancestral seat of Abdullah Husayn Al Ahmar, the influential sheikh of the Hashid confederation and former chairman of the advisory council. His brother Abdurahman Muhammad, president of the LDA in Khamir, took part in the above mentioned gathering.

Al Hamdi's role in the establishment of CYDA is not clearly evident. Being president of an LDA and also a cabinet member, he was serving two masters. The interest of the "central authorities" in supervising and coordinating the activities of the LDAs is obvious. Whether indeed Al Hamdi was in concordance with government leaders and the cabinet, or perhaps seized the initiative by himself, is not clear. In consideration of the power struggle of the established politicians in 1972-1974, which partly led to the paralysis of government activities, it seems likely that Al Hamdi took the initiative as an energetic politician during the first year of his political career.

The first CYDA conference, in which 26 LDA representatives participated, took place on 25th June, 1973. The conference attracted considerable attention from the highest political level, which is documented by the participation of high ranking government officials during the opening session. The election of an administrative council consisting of 15 members with Al Hamdi as president, as well as the promulgation of the CYDA charter, were the most important results of the first conference.[20]

In analyzing the significance of the founding of CYDA and the first conference, it is important to study its subsequent development.

For this purpose, it is necessary to explain a government resolution which was passed in time for the first conference. The LDAs were to receive immediately 25% of the Zakat revenue and 25% of the local administrations' income (baladiya) "for the execution of local projects (...) under the direct supervision of CYDA".[21] The government, in effect, gave the LDAs a part of its tax revenue as a relatively stable source of income making them less dependent on voluntary contributions. This decision was an indication of political foresight. Because of its economic and political weakness the government had to depend on the people's own initiatives. On the other hand, it is a well-known fact, that the government's Zakat revenue after the revolution constituted only a fraction of the estimated value of agricultural production.[22] By relinquishing a part of the Zakat revenue to the LDAs for financing local development projects, the government succeeded in raising the tax morale considerably. Thus the revenue from Zakat multiplied between 1973-1976, while the agricultural production hardly increased.[23]

With CYDA an instrument was created which allowed the coordination of the different LDA projects, as well as centrally planned activities. The government also obtained potential influence on the LDAs through CYDA, since these had to use government contributions under the supervision of CYDA. Beyond that, at the CYDA general assembly, a panel was formed in which representatives from all over Yemen could come together to discuss their development problems. CYDA constituted an important link between the government and remote regions, with the potential of influencing the political and administrative system of the country,[24] which should come to fruition later on.

After the first conference, a wave of new LDA establishments followed, and their number doubled within a year.[25] Apart from CYDA and government campaigns, the fact that many sheikhs now emerged as leaders of LDAs might have been another reason for this development.

The Second Conference of CYDA

The second conference took place in Sana'a from November 10-13, 1974. Besides representatives from the 65 LDAs, the entire political leadership took part in this conference.[26]

The second conference was of extraordinary importance because of its inner-political impact. The events of June 13 had happened just five months before, and overshadowed the conference session.

When Al Hamdi took over on 13th June, 1974 as head of a seven member leadership council, the unresolved conflict between the representatives of tribal interests on one hand, and nationally oriented politicians on the other hand, had brought national politics to a virtual standstill. The composition of the leadership council reflected the conflicting interests: four of the seven members could be classified as tribal representatives. At the end of June, Al Hamdi increased the number of members of the leadership council to ten, in order to balance the predominance of the tribal representatives and thereby strengthened his position in relation to the tribes shortly after the take-over. In May and June of 1975 he dismissed all of the tribal representatives from the leadership council one after the other. He dissolved the advisory council in October of the same year, thereby depriving Al Ahmar, who was the council's president, of his most important post. With this move he had temporarily secured his power.[27]

What is the connection existing between these events and the second conference of CYDA? Al Hamdi made influential sheikhs his enemies, something he could only risk if he created his own power base. The army was one supporting leg after he had cleaned it from tribal influence, increasing their pay, improving training, and introducing measures of modernization.[28] The other supporting leg was to be the LDAs, which he hoped would become a mass mobilization in his favor. The second conference took place during a period in which Al Hamdi had effected a change in the government's balance of power in his favor. To that end, he wanted to secure his support through the LDAs.

In his opening speech, he expounded the following points:[29] the LDAs should play an avant-garde role; they would have to show the government the right way to development; the work of the LDAs would only be successful if it was "free from political moods and arguments", able to choose its own path. In connection with this, he furiously attacked "groups" (ba'd al-majmu'at) handling the funds of the LDAs as if they were their personal property. CYDA and the Ministry of Social Affairs, Youth and Labor would recognize only those LDAs as legitimate whose president and members had been freely elected. This was to protect the LDAs "from unrestrained personal interests". The following proclamation of a government resolution increased the LDAs' share of the state's Zakat from 25% to 50%. Because of his present function as chairman of the leadership council and in line with his view that political arguments should not impede the work of the LDAs, Al Hamdi announced his resignation as president of CYDA.

Despite this speech, he did not keep the LDAs out of the political conflicts, something he repeatedly alleged to do. On the contrary, he carefully developed the LDAs as a new political force on the political scene. His promise to hold free elections for the LDA panel aroused great hopes among the people. He himself had probably hoped that through these elections the sheikhs would be eliminated from the LDAs. The conference did not accept his offer of resignation, but demanded that he should stay in office. It is obvious that he wanted to assure himself of the support of the LDAs before starting the clean-up campaign in the army and the leadership council. Therefore, his offer of resignation was a tactical maneuver comparable to the "vote of confidence" in parliamentary democracies. At the second conference, the LDAs and CYDA became a political force offering strong support for Al Hamdi

The Cooperative Movement in Yemen

during his time in office. The LDAs, beyond their tremendous economic importance, by then also took up a political role with an impact on the balance of power in Yemen.

The agenda of the second conference dealt essentially with the lack of a uniform and binding organizational structure of the LDAs for the whole country. The conference demanded that the government and CYDA accelerate the passing of a new LDA law, thereby taking into consideration a range of proposals. The most important of these was the institutionalization of a general assembly which should consist of elected representatives of the people. Moreover, the conference requested Al Hamdi to instruct the different state organs not to interfere with the work of the LDAs.[30]

The Legislative Framework of the LDAs

In line with the resolutions of the second conference, the work of the LDAs was to be reorganized according to a new unified standard for the entire republic. In 1975, the government passed Law No.35[31] instructing CYDA and the Ministry of Social Affairs, Youth and Labor to prepare a new charter for the LDAs, CYDA, and the newly created coordination councils.

Law No.35

Law No.35 regulates in 30 articles all the affairs of the LDAs. It is divided into the three large sections of "Establishment and Goals", "Administration and Finance" and "Final Regulations".

The law designates the general assembly as the highest organ of an LDA. Every 500 inhabitants send one representative to the assembly (Art.9). The general assembly elects from its ranks an administrative council consisting of five to nine members, depending on whether it involves an LDA at sub-district, district or provincial level (Art.13). The administrative council has the function of electing the president and the general secretary of the LDA who, like the administrative council, are elected for a period of three years (Art.14).

The resources of the LDAs are basically divided into centralized and decentralized sources. Decentralized sources are those that the LDA receives as donations within its territory. Among those are the LDAs' share of 50% of the Zakat revenue, 25% of the local administrative income, 5 Rial membership dues per eligible voter, as well as voluntary contributions and donations (Art.17). The centralized financial sources are those which are distributed by CYDA, such as foreign aid, and a special duty of 2% levied on certain imported items for the benefit of the LDAs (Art.17).

The law also specifies the duties of the LDAs in regard to their finances (Art.18-20), the dissolution of an LDA (Art.22-25), and sanctions to be imposed when this or any other law is violated.

The LDA Charter

The LDA charter[32] which was formulated according to Law No.35, served the purpose of placing the work of the LDAs on a uniform legislative basis binding for all LDAs. The various charters which the LDAs had given themselves previously were to be dissolved.[33]

The standardized charter of the LDAs comprises 34 articles divided into five sections: definitions, general assembly, administrative council, source of finance, general regulations.

Basically, the charter contains all the points already laid down in Law No.35. The charter deals with the interpretation of the individual articles, whereby particularly the duties, rights and responsibilities of the various LDA organs are defined. The only new item is the election of an accountant by the administrative council according to Art.17. The executive committee of the LDA is thus composed of three people: the president, the secretary general, and an accountant. In the same article, it is specified that the president and the secretary general should hold their posts as their main professional activity.

The Charter of the Coordination Council

The coordination council is formed by the presidents of the LDAs working in the respective province. Its chairman is, by virtue of his office, the governor of the province (Art.1). The coordination council furthermore elects from its ranks a secretary general and an assistant, who is in charge of the day to day business (Art.2). The main duty of the coordination council is to mediate between the LDAs and CYDA. Furthermore, it is responsible for coordinating the various projects within the province, especially in the case of joint ventures by various LDAs (Art.8). Noteworthy is Art.17, according to which the coordination council can appoint a committee to take over the administration of an LDA whose administrative organs have been dismissed by its general assembly.

The CYDA Charter

The new CYDA charter[34] replaced the charter which was adopted at the first conference. In 17 Articles it regulates membership, responsibilities, financing and organizational structure.

A member of CYDA is any LDA who satisfies the regulations of Law No.35 (Art.3). The main responsibility is the promotion of LDA development projects. Moreover, CYDA should support the LDAs in obtaining the finances guaranteed to them by law, coordinate and supervise the various proposed projects, as well as supervise the administration and finances of the LDAs. It also represents the LDAs on the national and the international levels (Art.4-11).

Articles 9-13 lie at the core of the new charter, stipulating rules concerning the general assembly and the administrative council. The elected representatives of the LDAs form the general assembly which, in secret ballot, elects 11 of the 32 members of the administrative council. The secretary generals of the coordination councils elected on province-level provide 11 more members. The remaining 10 members come from the various service-related ministries. The administrative council elects from its ranks a secretary general and his assistants, whereas the presidency of CYDA is taken by the President of the Republic.

The structures for the reorganization of the LDAs elaborated in 1974 and 1975 comprise essentially the principles which Al Hamdi proclaimed in his opening speech at the second conference:
- The activities of the LDAs should be placed on a broad basis and be supported by the entire population.
- A modern and unified administration should make the work of the LDAs more effective and facilitate control over them (especially in checking corruption).

With the announcement of free elections, Al Hamdi succeeded in mobilizing support among the people. His popularity reached a climax in 1974 and 1975 and brought him close to being a charismatic leader. With this support, it was possible for him to carry through the elimination of the tribal representatives in the leadership council and the army.

However, he was less successful in the fight against corruption. The complicated system of mutual control mechanisms which is laid down in Law No.35 and the various charters, did not function as expected. This is not surprising considering the gap between intentions and actual abilities of the administration. There is no doubt that CYDA, the coordination council, and the LDAs were completely overtasked with the execution and supervision of their intended duties.[35]

As a matter of fact, a bureaucratic apparatus was created that ran contrary to the framework of the LDAs which were originally based on the idea of self-help. Moreover, the government's massive influence upon the internal affairs of the

LDAs, coupled with generous promises of support, is one of the reasons which led to a welfare-state mentality on part of the people, paralyzing their will for self-help.

The First General Elections

The first general elections of the LDA boards were held between the beginning of July and the middle of September, 1975.[36] They took place in three phases:
a) The people, according to Law No.35, elected a representative for every 500 inhabitants to the general assembly of the LDA.
b) The general assembly elected the administrative council consisting of between five and nine members. This council in turn elected the president and the secretary general.
c) The presidents of the LDAs formed the coordination council on the provincial level. It elected from its ranks a secretary general and his assistants.

The execution of the elections was entrusted to the Ministry of Social Affairs, Youth and Labor, and CYDA. They formed a "Supreme Election Committee" which was responsible for the preparation and execution of the elections on a national level. This committee established branches in the entire republic which were to supervise the elections. In August, extra committees were sent out to deal with potential denunciations of the elections and protests by the people.[37]

During the election of the general assembly, the problem of the great variation in competence of the individual LDAs had to be taken into consideration first, which varied greatly between the sub-district and province levels. In accordance with the election law, election delegates were chosen on rural, sub-district and district levels till the respective - not standardized - level of the LDA was reached, wherefrom the election according to the charter could proceed.

The election was by and large a great success which, to a certain degree, was to be attributed to the month-long media campaign to mobilize the people, initiated by Al Hamdi. For the first time in the history of Yemen, the election of representatives was not confined to definite groups, but drew the entire population with all its classes and levels. This will be rightly considered as one of the most important achievements of the "cooperative movement".[38] Difficult to answer is the question of whether the elections did succeed in removing the sheikhs from the LDA boards, which was Al Hamdi's declared goal. The names of the elected representatives suggest that in the southern provinces one hardly came across sheikhs in the administrative councils. In the north, old sheikh families predominantly won the race, allegedly partly through manipulations.[39] Still, one can view these first general elections as a climax of the democratic development in the years from 1973 to 1975. This development was also reflected in a free press, comparable even to the open Western media.

Al Hamdi himself, in spite of the success, did not seem completely satisfied with the election results. In his assessment of the elections,[40] there were indications that he felt the mobilization of the people went too far. It seems as if he was afraid of being by-passed by the people's will for democracy.

The Third CYDA Conference

The third CYDA conference took place from 23-25 November, 1975 in Taiz. More than three hundred representatives from 130 LDAs took part, and each LDA was represented by its elected president and secretary general.

Almost the entire political leadership, as well as representatives of foreign aid organizations took part in the opening session. Most important among the 18 prepared resolutions[41] were the new charters for LDAs and coordination council, and a demand for a review of the new CYDA charter taking into consideration the amendments proposed during the conference.

The significance of the third conference lay in the fact that, for the first time, the participants were representatives elected by the people who not only discussed the affairs of the LDAs but also the general situation of the country in all its political, social, and economic aspects.[42] In that sense, the general assembly of the third conference was similar the role of a parliament in Western democracies.

In his opening address, Al Hamdi stressed that the conference was an assembly of all social classes. Contrary to his speech at the second conference, where he emphasized the differences of the various social classes and furiously attacked the sheikhs in particular, he now stressed the need for "common service to the people and Fatherland" by all social classes.

The election at the conference of the eleven members of the CYDA administrative council led to a clash. According to reports of conference observers, Al Hamdi proposed a number of politicians and governors agreeable to him as candidates, but these were all rejected by the general assembly. Instead, "a group of young, conscious and sincere people" emerged from the elections as winners.[43] The remaining 10 of the 21 members of the administrative council were elected by the coordination councils shortly after the conference. At the constitutional session, Al Hamdi was again elected president of CYDA. However, Abdalhafiz Bahran, supposedly leaning to the left, was elected secretary general, succeeding the rather conservative Abdullah Al Halali. The result of the election of the

The Local Development Associations

administrative council showed that the people were not willing to follow the political leadership blindly.

On the other hand, Al Hamdi's changed attitude has become obvious. "In autumn of 1975, he turned away from his favorite "stalagmite" mobilization model to his now established "stalactite" undertaking. In speeches and official statements, as well as in the state controlled media, the newly created "corrective movement" (al-haraka at-tashihiya) now occupied the place of the cooperative movement (al-haraka at-ta'awuniya). The sphere of activities of its committees and sub-committees, which were constituted from the top, were the authorities, public enterprises, and educational establishments in the country, far removed from the concerns of the rural population."[44] With the third conference, the institutional development of the LDAs reached their provisional climax and conclusion. Law No.35 and the charters based on it formed the legislative basis of the LDAs. In less than 2 years, the LDAs and CYDA have become a force on the national level, which plays an important role in neutralizing traditional tribal influence.

1   Ash-Shaiba: At-Tatawwur at-tashri'i fi harakatina at-ta'awuniya, in Al-Ghad, Nr.12/1978,S.78
2   Al-Jarida ar-rasmiya, Nr.8, Sana'a 1963, S.80-84
3   Ash-Shaiba 1978, p.79
4   Marriot, P.C.: Cooperative activity in the Yemen Arab Republic, in: Yearbook of Agricultural Cooperation. Oxford 1972, p.151
5   Al-Harbi: Zahirat at-ta'awun al-ahli lit-tatwir wa-atharuha fit-tanmiya al-yamaniya, in: Al-Ghad, Nr.10/1978, p.19
6   Al-Ittihad al-'am li-hai'at at-ta'awun al-ahli lit-tatwir (CYDA): Kitab at-ta'awun, Nr.1, Sana'a 1974, p.11
7   Al-Azzazi, M.: Al-Masadir al-maliya li-hai'at at-ta'awun al-ahli, in: Al-Ghad,Nr.4 1977,p.45
8   Al-Alimi, A.M.: At-Ta'awun...qudr wa-masir, in: Al-Ghad, Nr.11 1978,p.14
9   Halliday, F.: Arabia without Sultans, Harmondsworth/USA 1974,p.122
10   Halliday 1974, p.119
11   Hai'at tatwir Al-Hujariya; Thalath sanawat min al-bina', p.9
12   ibidem p.24
13   Al-Ittihad 1974, p.14

14	Art.11 from the constitution of 1964
15	Al-Ittihad al-'am 1974, pp.12
16	Al-Ittihad 1974, p.14
17	ibidem p.17
18	ibidem p.15
19	see also Al-Ittihad 1974, p.18
20	see also Al-Ittihad 1974, pp.38-48
21	Al-Ittihad 1974, p.80
22	in 1972-73 only some 25% of the possible Zakat income reached the treasury (Al-Azzazi 1977,pp.74)
23	World Bank: Yemen Arab Republic, Development of a traditional economy, Washington D.C. 1979, Tab.5.2 and 7.3
24	Azzazi: Die Entwicklung der Arabischen Republik Jemen, Tubingen 1978,p.164
25	Al-Mu'ayyad: Al-Haraka at-ta'awuniya, Kitab at-ta'awun, Nr.6, Sana'a, p.19
26	Al-Ittihad: Kitab at-ta'wun, Nr.2, Sana'a 1975, p.2
27	see also Koszinowski, El-Menshaui, Meyer: Zur politischen und wirtschaftlichen Situation im Jemen, Hamburg 1980, pp.20
28	ibidem
29	Al-Ittihad 1975, pp.4-10
30	ibidem
31	Al-Ittihad: Kitab at-ta'wun, Nr.3, Sana'a pp.29-41
32	ibidem, pp.49-65
33	ibidem, p.48
34	Al-Ittihad al-'am: Kitab, Nr.7, Sana'a 1979, pp.346-354
35	Azzazi 1978, p.163
36	Al-Ittihad: at-ta'awun, Nr.54, 26.9.1975, p.4
37	Al-Ittihad: at-ta'awun, Nr.48, 16.7.1975, p.8
38	Al-'Audi, Kitab al-Ghad, Nr.4, Sana'a 1978, p.38
39	Al-'Audi, 1978, p.40
40	speech from 20.10.1977 in front of the Administrative Board of CYDA
41	Al-Ittihad: Kitab, Nr.3, p.26
42	Al-Ghad, Nr.4/1977, pp.15
43	Al-'Audi: Kitab Al-Ghad, Nr.2, Sana'a 1977, p.119
44	Kruse: Verwaltungsentwicklung

The Cooperative Movement of Yemen: Developments after 1985

by Fritz Piepenburg

The Political Setting for the Rise of the Cooperative Movement

The political events of the 1960ies caused tremendous change in both parts of Yemen. In the northern part, the death of Imam Ahmad and the republican revolution conducted by the military on September 26, 1962, marked the dawn of a new age. In the south, the first organized revolt against a police station manned with British personnel in Habilayn, at the foot of the Radfan mountains, on October 14, 1963 became the triggering point of the battle for independence. Yet, before liberation and independence could actually be enjoyed, both parts had to wage bitter civil wars: the republicans in the north against the forces of Imam Muhammad Badr, who managed to escape after his overthrow, and the liberation movements in the south against the British colonial power. Both wars were fierce and cruel at times. During the 70-day siege of Sana'a at the end of 1967, the republicans were fighting for their bare survival. In the south, entire villages were subjected to punitive air raids by units of the British air force stationed in Aden.

With the British withdrawal from Aden on November 30, 1967, colonialism in the southern part of Yemen came to a sudden end. The war in the northern part lasted even longer, until a final compromise was elaborated between the republicans and the royalists during a meeting of Islamic foreign ministers in March 1970 in Jeddah, Saudi Arabia. Real development could only commence from then on. And it happened by leaps and bounds. People suddenly became aware of the world around them and the fact that they were living in the 20th century. A feeling of relief from a heavy and backward past and a sense of new beginning spread throughout the country and reached even remote villages. The marvels of the 20th century, such as piped water, electricity, roads, motorized vehicles, etc. found widespread admiration. And what is even more important, people became increasingly capable of affording these luxuries thanks to the savings of their brethren working in oil-rich neighboring countries.

Thus, the background was set for launching multifaceted activities of cooperation. The atmosphere was especially conductive in former North Yemen, where the government initially gave a great deal of freedom to the private sector, limiting its involvement to charging fees for granting import licences. - The situation was somewhat different in the south, where large-scale nationalization was carried out by the government under Salem Ali Rubay'a which, on June 22, 1969 launched the so-called "corrective step". The situation in former South Yemen shall be dealt with in a later chapter.

The Zeal and Enthusiasm of the Early Cooperatives

The roots of the cooperative movement in the northern part were spontaneous, inspired by the people themselves, and full of zeal and enthusiasm. People caught in its spirit displayed a remarkable degree of willingness to sacrifice all available means - be they financial, in kind, or through the provision of skills - for the sake of communal development. Cooperatives first appeared in Mokha and Al-Hujjariyah, and their number quickly rose from 28 in 1973 to 164 in 1975. Old concepts of cooperation were revived and villages, freed from the yoke of fear of the Imam and relieved from the suffering of the civil war, remembered their inherent strength and capabilities. By planning projects that required the cooperation of several villages, old barriers of former isolation were broken down. Indigenous skills and expertise rose high in demand and were readily shared by everybody.

On the economic level, people developed a remarkable capability of raising their own funds. Local material and expertise were utilized to the fullest extent, and beneficiaries from a certain project voluntarily contributed over 50% of the total costs. Planning and supervision of the projects were done with utmost care and concern, since the projects were the people's own ideas and money. There was little room for carelessness or sloppy work, because the inhabitants were doing things in their own interest. Nobody felt tempted to steal or misuse funds, since everybody had contributed his own share and wanted the project to succeed.

A comprehensive paper on the cooperative movement compiled by the Ministry of Local Administration in 1991, states that projects (no matter if it was the construction of a road, the provision of running water, electrification, the building of schools or health units) done by the cooperatives were 40 to 50% less expensive than the projects implemented by the government.[1]

On the political level, the spirit of cooperation fostered a spread of democratic behavior. A cooperative would elect from its active membership the most capable person to become its president. It was then up to the president to ensure that progress was being achieved, even if pressure had to be applied to the government offices concerned with the provision of the necessary licenses and permits. The work speed and enthusiasm of the local cooperatives made it difficult for the central government to catch up and keep pace. Because of these cooperatives, a sense of community transcending traditional boundaries of class, of clans and tribes, was created, paving the way for the final goal of developing a sense of nation-building.

The Challenges of the late 70ies and early 80ies

The sporadic development of the cooperatives in the former YAR was both, an opportunity and a challenge to the central government. There was a tremendous opportunity to quickly popularize the central government and build an understanding of nationhood among the people by carefully coordinating and supporting the spread of the cooperatives. The challenge clearly lay in the understandable desire of the government to exercise some measure of control and direction over these self-help communities. Taking control over and trying to influence the direction of the movement, however, had to be done with extreme caution and sensitivity, if the self-generated momentum of the cooperatives and the zeal and enthusiasm of its members were to be preserved. Forming a delicate and workable balance between the legitimate claim of the government to know what was happening in the various parts of the nation and to exercise a certain measure of influence on these events, while carefully preserving the feeling of the people that they continued to realize their own decisions, must have been a tremendous challenge to the young national leadership. It shall be seen in the following chapters of this paper, how well the government was able to cope with this challenge.

The government of Ibrahim Al-Hamdi (1974-1977) apparently understood that the best way of obtaining government control over the cooperatives was by centrally coordinating their activities and providing government assistance, expertise, and finance. By initializing a process of systematic elections for the cooperatives all the way up to the national level, he fostered the growth of a democratic awareness among the people and himself rose to a high level of popularity. Unfortunately, Al-Hamdi's path of nation-building and democratization came to a sudden end with his untimely and brutal assassination.

After the short-lived government of Hassan Al-Ghashmi (assassinated in June 1978), the newly elected head of state Ali Abdullah Saleh was also elected President of the Confederation of Yemeni Development Associations (CYDA), like Al-Hamdi before him. The cooperatives continued to thrive until the early 80ies, when a number of problems began to arise. Problems listed in the aforementioned paper[2] include the lack of adequate technical supervision, the misuse of public funds (certain projects apparently were only existing on paper for the purpose of collecting contributions), conflicting laws and regulations between different LDAs and the ascent of LDA leadership personalities who had no sense for public service, but were merely seeking to enhance their own political image. The worst of all problems was the lack of clearly defined rights and responsibilities of the LDAs. Other public organizations, such as the Municipal Councils, the Local Administrative Councils, and others tended to interfere squarely into the realm of responsibility originally allotted to the cooperatives. People lost faith in their own associations and began withdrawing their support. Something needed to be done urgently to remedy the situation, if public support for the cooperatives was to be preserved. This remedy was to be Law No.12 of 1985.

Law No.12 of 1985

The task at hand was clearly defined: the cooperatives were to be reorganized from the very bottom by conducting nation-wide elections for so-called Local Councils for Cooperative Development (LCCD), the successors of the LDAs. The legal framework was to be provided by Law No.12, which specified the rules for the creation of the new cooperatives.

Only three months after the law had been passed, nation-wide elections for forming the LCCDs took place. Participation turned out to be high. The two election days of July 17 and 18 were declared a public holiday. Some 5 Million Yemenis, including women, went to the polls to elect their representative to the LCCD. These were the first free and democratic elections held in modern North Yemen. A total of 209 general assemblies of LCCDs were elected, consisting of 21 to 110 members each, the exact number being determined by the density of population. The elections were carefully prepared by an able election committee and went very smoothly. Mosques, schools, and other public buildings temporarily served as polling stations.

Typically, one elected member stood for an electorate of 500 people. The Local Council normally covered the population within a given district (nahiyah). Districts with an extremely high population could have more than one Local Council. Members of the general assembly (GA) were elected for a six-year term in office.

The general assembly then elected from among its members a chairman and the administrative board (AB) numbering between 7 and 11 persons for a three-year term in office. They, in turn, chose among themselves the secretary general and a financial officer. The chairman of the general assembly was also the chairman of the administrative board. The board met at least once a month and acted as the administrative body of the Local Council. It prepared draft programs and projects, undertook activities related to rent, sales, and contracts, and prepared the draft budget to be presented to the general assembly at least twice a year together with a detailed report of activities.

The elections turned out to be a full success. President Saleh himself called them "an important step in the direction of democracy ... and a bold strategy to hand over more responsibility to the general public."[3] As a matter of fact, they became a valuable testing ground for nation-wide parliamentary elections that should take place 3 years later on July 5, 1988. However, the exact function of the newly elected Councils and their correlation with the various service-related ministries was not clear at all. It was Law No.27 of the same year that clarified those important details.

Law No.27 of 1985 and Subsequent Developments

Law No.27 of 1985 basically transferred a great deal of responsibility and power to the provincial governors (muhafidh) and district directors (mudir an-nahiah). The LCCDs were required to coordinate all of their projects and activities with the government represented by the Executive Council (EC), which consisted of top administrators of the respective administrative unit and was chaired by the governor or the district director respectively. An important problem to be solved was the question of how to connect the democratic basis at the bottom (the LCCDs) with the organization representing the central government at the top (the ECs). This link between the LCCDs and the ECs was to be the Coordination Council (CC). The CC was charged with coordinating and integrating LCCD initiatives with government projects and policies at both administrative levels. It consisted of high-ranking officials from the EC and the chairmen of the LCCDs and was chaired by the governor or the director respectively.

The decision to place much of the affairs of the LCCDs under the supervision of the governor and other government officials turned out to be detrimental, if not fatal, to the spirit of self-help and private initiative. In the words of the report compiled by the Ministry of Local Administration[4], "it caused the Local Councils to become democratic organizations without any real power to create, or administer, or generate projects beyond the firm control of the state executive power. The Local Councils were in fact transformed from financially and administratively independent organizations into an apparatus participating in the execution of the orders of government officials." - Decision-making powers were placed almost exclusively into the hands of the governor and, at the next subordinate level, to the district directors, all appointed by the central government without requesting the participation of the local population.

The massive government encroachment on the LCCDs didn't stop here. Before 1988, the LCCDs were centrally coordinated and supported by the Confederation of the LCCDs with seat in Sana'a. The CLCCD traditionally was chaired by the President of the Republic and consisted of a general congress and the administrative board. The general congress was composed of all LCCD chairmen and no less than three members of every administrative board of each LCCD. It convened every 3 years. The administrative board of the Confederation was traditionally headed by the President of the Republic and consisted of both elected and appointed individuals. The general congress elected 20 of its members to serve in the administrative board. In addition, a number of high government officials became automatically part of the board, such as the Ministers of Development, Interior, and Finance; the Chairman of the Central Agency for Accounting and Auditing; deputies from the ministries of education, health, municipalities and housing, social affairs and labor, public works, electricity and water, transport, Awqaf, and information.

Until 1988, the secretary general of the CLCCD and his assistant were elected by the 20 elected members of the administrative board from among themselves, and held the rank of a minister and a deputy minister. Beginning with 1988, the secretary general and his assistant received the rank of a minister and a deputy minister, and were by the government. The Confederation changed its name into the General Secretariat of the LCCDs (GSLCCD). After the unification of the northern and southern parts of the Republic of Yemen in May, 1990, the GSLCCD was renamed into the Ministry of Local Administration, headed by the Minister of Local Administration. The Deputy for the Sector of Local Councils became the main government representative for the Local Councils.

In a move which might be considered brilliant by political strategists, all elected representatives of the LCCDs automatically became members of the People's General Congress, the political organization of the government in power. This led to a further politicization of the Local Councils. The results of these policies did not come as a surprise. Issues of local development became confused with politics and political strategies. Funds from the LCCD budgets were occasionally used for political purposes. The elected members of the LCCDs became disenchanted to the point, where they would not even attend the general assemblies. People in general became reluctant to pay the fees for their Local Councils. The local authorities reacted with threats of arrest and imprisonment. The LCCDs began to face an increased burden of debts, but nobody really felt responsible for them. An official estimate puts the total debt of the LCCDs at YR 85 Million by the end of 1989.[5]

Despite these grave problems, figures for the accomplishments of the LCCDs between 1987 and 1989 are somewhat impressive. However, the figures given below do not differentiate between new construction and maintenance, and thus it is difficult to evaluate them as proof of real development.

New Construction and Maintenance of LCCD Projects[6]
(1987 - 1989)

Roads (km)	21,548	YR 126,512,094
School Class Rooms	6,479	176,970,869
Health Units	589	79,776,213
Water Supply	755	105,402,810
Other Projects	845	93,447,401
Total:		**YR 582,109,387**

The paper drafted by the Ministry of Local Administration recommends the adoption of a number of measures, all aiming at the restoration of the original popularity and trust the cooperatives originally enjoyed among the people.[7] Complete independence, politically and economically, was to be restored, freeing the LCs from excessive government interference and returning some of their original vigor and energy. The original relationship between the LC and the local government offices needed to be restored in such a way that the offices became a help and support for the projects devised and implemented by the LC, not a burden. All LCs should be freed from their heavy debts, allowing them to make a new beginning. The LC should no longer be required to run and maintain past projects, such as health units and schools, allowing the accumulation of capital for new projects. - These recommendations were given prior to the passing of Law No.52 of 1991, which provides new regulations for the Local Councils, replacing the two previous laws of 1985. Law No.52 will be dealt with in detail, following the next chapter on the Cooperative Movement in the southern part of Yemen.

Cooperatives in the Southern Part

The administrative division in the southern part was done in the form of 6 provinces (muhafadha), which were further divided into 30 directorates (mudiriyah), and 95 centers (markaz). A system of local governments was established on the provincial and directorate levels, called the People's Local Councils. In 1976/77, local elections were held for the first time in the province of Hadhramawt, and then in the other provinces. Some 204 members were elected, among them 21 women. Members were elected to a 2-year term in office. A total of 8 PLCs came into existence (one in each province and two additional ones in Radfan and Sayun/Hadhramawt). Later on, elections were also organized to create PLCs on the level of the directorates. The Councils were charged with directing local affairs in the economic, social, and cultural fields. They were closely coordinating their efforts with other mass organizations (esp. the unions), state-owned collective farms, and cooperatives.

From the very beginning, the PLCs received tough competition from the so-called Popular Defence Committees (PDC). These Committees were first established in Sheikh Othman (near Aden) in 1973, taking their inspiration from the Cuban example. More PDCs were then quickly established in other major cities and, to a lesser degree, in the countryside as well. The basic unit was at the level of the neighborhood, with higher leadership bodies being formed at the directorate, province, and finally national levels. From the very beginning, the PDCs were closely supervised and directed by the ruling party (YSP) and functioned as an important communication link between the leadership and the people at "grass-roots level". Among the original tasks allocated to the PDCs were night time security checks of the neighborhoods, organizing volunteer work for cleaning public places, and maintaining/renovating public buildings, distributing ration cards and basic food supplies, organizing anti-illiteracy and health campaigns, controlling local housing and solving simple family and social problems. In practice, however, the security function and the passing on of party policies tended to dominate the work of the PDCs.

The cooperatives established in the former PDRY, of course, followed the socialist model, and therefore had little in common with the cooperative movement of the former YAR. After the overthrow of President Qahtan Al-Sha'bi by Salem Ali Rubay'a on June 22, 1969 (the so-called corrective step), large-scale nationalization of foreign banks and private companies got underway. The second Agrarian Reform Law (issued on November 5, 1970) actively encouraged peasants to take over the land from the large land owners by force. The state itself confiscated all the land owned by sultans and sheikhs, as well as the religious endowment (waqf), without paying any compensation. Private land holding was limited to 40 feddans of irrigated land or 80 feddans of rain-fed land per family.

Three forms of agricultural organizations emerged, perceived by the theorists as following each other as stages of development in realizing socialism. In the first stage, individuals within the cooperatives kept their own holdings, while managing irrigation, the operation of machinery, and the provision of fertilizer and seeds collectively (production sharing cooperatives). In the second stage, individual lands were joined and work carried out collectively (service sharing cooperatives). After the deduction of costs, profits were to be distributed among the peasants according to land and labor contribution. In cooperatives of the third stage, all land and services were owned by the cooperative. Profits were distributed solely on the basis of labor contribution.[8]

While this model may have appeared convincing to the Marxist scholar, the actual result was quite different. Among the 44 agricultural cooperatives that came into existence until 1980, most remained in the first or second stage. The production sharing cooperatives turned out to be the most efficient ones.

State owned farms represented another form of agricultural organization. Laborers were treated the same as other employees, receiving fixed wages and additional bonuses for net profits. According to a World Bank survey done in 1977, the state farms were the least efficient. Even though the government had invested YD 34 million between 1971 and 1977 (22% of all development investments) the yearly production figures for crops actually declined.[9]

Better results were achieved in the sector of fishery. Following the "corrective step", boats, gear and other fishing instruments were nationalized and the distribution of the catch placed under government control. By 1977, some 7,500 fishermen were organized in 14 cooperatives and placed under the authority of the Ministry of Fish Wealth. The government spent YD 22.8 million (40% of all development investments) in the sector of fishery. The ministry acquired a new fleet, primarily for the purpose of increasing exports. Joint ventures were undertaken with the former Soviet Union, and fishing concessions sold to Japanese firms. Fishery became more important to the national income than agriculture and livestock breeding combined. By 1977, fish and fish meal amounted to 60% of all commodities exported from the PDRY.[10]

Other cooperatives were established under the Cooperative Law of 1972, such as cooperatives for consumers, social services, livestock and crafts. Policies under President Ali Nasser Muhammad (who took over from Ismael Ali Fatah on April 20, 1980) were pragmatic, and granting more liberty to the farmers and fishermen working in the cooperatives.[11]

The Situation after National Unification

The emergence of the Republic of Yemen on 22 May, 1990 demanded the unification of the systems of Local Councils in the northern and southern parts. While the administrative division on the first level was the same in both parts of the country (province - muhafadhah), divisions on subsequent levels bore different names. It was decided by the new government to accept the name "directorate" (mudiriyah) for the next administrative level. Thus, the former districts (nahiah) of the northern part were renamed into directorates. The exact borders of the directorates and their further subdivisions are still awaiting their final definition by a law to be issued in the near future.

Law No.52 of 1991[11] reorganizes the Local Councils[12] on two levels: the level of the province and the level of the directorate. The basic emphasis of the law is to link the LCs with the policies promulgated by the central government. Administrative units and Local Councils are part of the state authority, supervised and directed by the Council of Ministers through the Ministry of Local Administration[13]. The LCs are to be elected by each administrative unit (the province as a whole and each directorate individually) and function for a period of 3 years. The LC on the provincial level has between 31 and 51 members, while 21 to 41 members form one LC on the directorate level. Each LC elects from its members a president, who, among other things, is also responsible for implementing the decisions taken by the Presidential Council and the Council of Ministers.

As was the case with the previous law, an Executive Council (EC) (one on each of the two administrative levels) is charged with preparing plans and proposals and overseeing the implementation of projects approved by the higher authorities. The EC is the ultimate body to decide on matters of public concern. The governor is the chairman of the EC on the provincial level, and the director on the level of the directorate. Other members include the deputy governor/deputy director, heads of government offices at the respective levels, the director of security, and the director of the diwan (Administrative Council). Quite surprisingly and contrary to the previous law, the new law makes no mention of a Coordination Council (CC), which formerly allowed the presidents of the LCs direct access to the Executive Councils. The interests of the LC are looked after by the "general director for matters relating to the LCs", who himself is part of the diwan. The LC is only empowered to submit proposals to the EC and receive regular reports from the EC's sessions.[14]

As with the previous law, the main thrust of the political power lies with the position of the provincial governor, and, to a lesser extent, with the directors of the directorates. The governor is to be appointed by the Presidential Council and approved by the Council of Ministers. He holds the rank of a minister. His many duties include the preparation of a yearly budget for the entire province and a yearly financial report (including the budgets of the LCs). He has to coordinate and supervise all government offices on the provincial level (with the exception of courts and other legal offices, which are subject to the Ministry of Justice only).

Among his impressive array of powers is the right to transfer any government employee at the level lower than general director, if he considers this person to be in conflict with the public purpose of the higher political directives. Concerning civil servants at the level of general director or higher, he has the right to ask the minister concerned to transfer the person to another post.[15]

The governor is in charge of security issues, the collection of fees, taxes, and even the Zakat (religious tax). He is responsible for guaranteeing an adequate supply of basic food commodities, and has to watch the development of prices. - These powers and responsibilities are reflected to a lesser degree in the authorities of the directors of the directorates, who are appointed by the Prime Minister and approved by the Council of Ministers.

Judging from the above mentioned regulations, the actual decision-making power granted to the LCs seems to be quite restrained. However, the law makes certain provisions which do give the LCs an important voice. All local development plans, programs, budgets, etc. need to be passed on to the LC for discussion and approval, before the governor can submit them to the central government. Members of the LC have the right to ask questions to heads of government departments (on the provincial or the directorate level). The government official in question has to answer in person or through a representative during the next meeting of the LC. In this regard, the LCs are given a function similar to that of the national parliament, on a local level. The term "small-scale parliament" to describe the LCs has been repeatedly used by high ranking officials of the MoLA.[16]

The LCs are able to pass their own decisions and resolutions, but the law explicitly mentions that they have to be within the framework of the overall state policies. Government offices can oppose a certain decision or resolution taken by the LC, and return it for revision. If the LC persists in its decision, the matter is forwarded to the minister concerned, who can again object to the decision and return it to the LC. If the LC again insists upon the original version of the resolution, it has to be forwarded to the Council of Ministers, which is required to discuss the matter within 30 days. The decision of the Council of Ministers is final and irreversible.

The detailed relationship between the democratically elected LCs and the government appointed ECs will be dealt with in the by-laws to be decided upon at a later date. Law No.52 in its entirety can only take effect after the completion of LC elections on both administrative levels, which will take place after national elections for parliament. Officials of the MoLA also mentioned the aspiration of the Ministry to expand the democratic basis of the local administration in the future, eventually leading to a stage, where the directors of the directorates and the governors of the provinces are being elected by the people of the respective administrative unit.

1. "Evaluation of the Cooperative Experiment" (taqiyim at-tajrubah at-ta'awuniyah) compiled by the Ministry of Local Administration on occasion of the joint meeting of the newly appointed Council of Ministers and the governors in 1991.
2. Ibid. pp 23-27
3. See also "Yemeni Local Council Elections - A Step towards Parliamentary Poll", in The Middle East Times, Vol. III No.31
4. "Evaluation of the Cooperative Experiment", p.34
5. Ibid. p.42
6. Ibid. P.46
7. Ibid. pp.53-56
8. "PDR Yemen. Politics, Economics and Society", by Tareq Y. Ismael and Jacqueline S. Ismael, London 1986 pp. 81-88
9. "People's Democratic Republic of Yemen. A Review of Economic and Social Development", The World Bank 1979
10. "South Yemen: A Marxist Republic in Arabia", by Robert W. Stookey, London 1982, pp. 83-84
11. The government of united Yemen is now in the process of re-privatizing the state cooperatives and the state owned farms.
11. Law No.52 of 1991, issued on April 25, 1991: "Law of Local Administration", published in "Al-Jaridah Al-Rasmiyah" (Official Gazette) Vol.8, April 30, 1991 by the Ministry of Legal Affairs
12. The new name Local Council is formed by taking the common words of the "Local Council for Cooperative Development" of the north and the "People's Local Council" from the south
13. Law No.52 of 1991, para. 4, 50, 58
14. Ibid. section 4,6
15. Ibid. para. 21
16. Conversation of the author with Ahmad Al-Harbi, Deputy Minister for the Sector of Local Councils, and Abdulbaqi Nu'man, Director for Public Relations, on August 15, 1992.

PART II:

Other Examples of Regional Development

The Non-aligned Economics of East African Villages

by Vivian Craddock Williams, Economist

Economists should be concerned with formulating practical policies for implementation by national governments and corporate managements; macro-economic policies for the first, and micro-economic for the second.

The origin of the word 'economics' in Greek is still conveyed in the best of current economic practice. The profession is addressed to the management of the 'Ecos', the natural and man-made environment, and like 'gnomes', should use preternatural skill and wisdom in doing so. Present-day economics is the good housekeeping of ancient Greece writ large.

The objective, always, is optimizing the flow of net benefits over time, lowering costs and increasing benefits for the nation state, or community neighborhood, or corporate enterprise, over whatever period the client chooses, whether for the very short term or for posterity over several generations.

Economics has developed useful tools for making the best of this job, all of them relating in some way to the concept of measuring efficiency through variations on the input/output ratio. The terms employed always, however, need to be defined with great precision if we are to achieve clarity, and avoid misunderstanding. If they are, they can be of the greatest use in designing effective policies whether for a village cooperative in East Africa or the national budget.

Rural Development and Industrialization

Policies for rural development are clearly very important for any country where more than half the total population lives outside the urban areas, and where most of the gross domestic product is generated by agriculture. Very serious consequences follow in countries dependent on rural output if the rains fail, or if rural policies are misdirected. And most countries in East Africa are of this sort. Over 80% of Ethiopia's population lives in the rural areas, though famine and drought have greatly accelerated urban drift, and nearly half the country's GDP is produced by agriculture.

In Kenya, which is rather more industrialized, the same proportion of people live in the rural areas, but a much higher proportion of the GDP is produced from industry and urban services.

In Zambia, which has an even greater industrial sector based on the country's copperbelt, only 55% of the people live in the rural areas; only 14% of the GDP is produced by agriculture, and 36% is produced by industry. But even here, much of the industry uses the output of agriculture as raw materials, and so the linkage between the two sectors is crucial to the economic prosperity of the country, and rural development is a national priority.

Comparative statistics are a valuable source of economic data in establishing workable policies. So from Table One, we can see that North Yemen, too, has a priority need for effective rural development policies. Over 80% of the people live outside the towns, and yet agriculture and rural industries contribute less than 26% of GDP. Saudi Arabia by contrast has urbanized rapidly: over 77% of GDP arises from industrial activity, including the oil industry, and at present only 1% of GDP comes from farming, though new policies and investments may increase this proportion to create a more balanced economy.

A fully industrialized country like the United Kingdom has over 90% of all its people living in urban areas, and derives only 2% of its GDP from agriculture. Villages in industrialized Europe have become little more than dormitories for workers commuting from them to the industrialized and business centers. Although we in Europe attach great sentimental value to village life, no one can pretend that villages have anything like the economic importance they have in East Africa, or in North Yemen.

Issues of Regional Development

The Village as the Key Unit for Development

Governments in East Africa recognize that the village represents a key unit in economic development. During the colonial era, and even now in many East African countries, the villages were small in size, and rather vulnerable to natural disaster. They were small because they were never settled enough to grow, and it seems that the natural birth and death rate of the village community maintained it in balance with the resources that were at its disposal. These villages were scattered probably because of tribal wars and slave trading, which required dispersal over a wide area, but also because the carrying capacity of the land in terms of hunting and farming potential was strictly limited. Although these villages were always vulnerable to drought and famine, because they never had the technologies for extensive irrigation and pest proof storage, they were at least invulnerable to inflation. Being largely self sufficient, their cash and import needs were limited to about 5 to 10% of their local community GDP. In other words, the typical East African village was by and large outside the modern cash economy: it consumed what it produced, and it grew cash crops, or traded animal trophies only in order to have enough cash to buy hoes, or cloth, or some other product not produced within the village.

The terms of trade has recently moved against the village economy. The unit prices of goods produced in the towns or imported from other countries have increased relative to the market value of the agricultural goods the village produces to pay for them. To buy a tractor in 1965, a Tanzanian village in 1965 only had to sell 20 bags of cashew nuts; but in 1985, a tractor costs them 52 bags. Similar examples have been quoted over time by the Tanzanian President, Julius Nyerere, in explaining his country's economic predicament. But sometimes the terms of trade move in favor of the village economy; for example, in Zambia butchers have paid increasing amount to obtain cattle for meat. Villagers on the Kafue Flats used to sell 150 cattle a year to meet their cash needs. With the increase in the price of cattle, they only needed to sell 136 cattle to earn enough to buy in the imports they needed from Lusaka, a nice example of the backward swinging supply curve.

Total self-help, or 100% self sufficiency has existed in very remote villages. But almost by definition it can be seen that such village life was deprived of some advantages, and must have been very limiting in scope.

Where material and spiritual needs are very simple, and are largely supplied by nature, with year round air conditioning, and fruit dropping from the trees, no one need exert himself very much, and the prevailing ethos is one of benign and easy going lassitude, and the total absence of development ambition.

Much more common was the evolution of the comparative advantages that one village could offer the next in the supply of goods and services. Classically, the exchanges possible through trade encouraged specialization, and lowered the cost of a wider variety of goods and services. It is of course precisely on such advantages that international trade and specialization has developed with lowered costs and increased gains for all nations that participate in it. In political terms, for defensive systems, and for the benefits of trade, East African villages forego anything like self-help and all look to mutual inter-dependence to some degree or other.

Positive correlations of trading pattern and ideological alignment need to be researched further. Both socialist and capitalist countries trade across national frontiers for mutual benefit, though clearly socialist countries within COMECON do so in a far more controlled way. Trading is largely a function of size, so that the larger an economy, whether a village or nation state, the more likely it is to be self-sufficient and independent of external supplies. The marked feature of East African village is that generally they are neither obviously socialist in structure nor are they obviously capitalist. They have the characteristics of both systems in varying degrees, and in a nice balance of collective and individualist interests which the Zambian President Kenneth Kaunda has termed Humanism, and which he has promoted as a distinctive African ideology since the early days of Zambia's United National Independence Party in the 1960s.

Economic rights and duties in the East African village have evolved over long periods of history without the benefit, if that is the right term, of theorists, ideologists or propagandists. Individuals within the village have traditional rights of control and use of economic assets, but this is balanced by the duty they have to share work and benefits with others in the community. Thus, the building of a house or the digging of a field and some urgent harvesting work would be typically and invariably collectivized, and so would to a lesser extent the sharing of stored feedstuffs and seed. As the village population would on average have been traditionally less than 500, it was always politically feasible to agree and organize village activities within a village council of less than say sixty heads of families. There could never be within an African village, east or west, a centralized power group acting in a socialist way to advance the interests of the whole community; nor could economic rights and privileges be appropriated and accumulated by a minority power group acting capitalistically against the interests of the whole community.

Social ties and obligations within the human scale of a village inhibit the development of these economic extremes, and of the theorizing that a larger economy is invariably created to support them. The village economy is an organic entity, not the construct of theorist. While there are notable exceptions to the general rule in any rural context subject to dynamic commercial forces, it is possible to discern in the East African village an economic practice that is ideologically non-aligned, neither socialist nor capitalist. Increasing number of economists working on the development of the non-aligned movement have identified features in it that represent efficient models for development in the larger economies of the nation states.

Government Intervention - Sensible and Sensitive

The intervention of governments in village life has been an inevitable consequence of the national need to increase agricultural output. The first means to that end was to provide infrastructure for villages engaged in farming so that output could be increased and transported out to earn foreign exchange. Since there were too many scattered villages, most of them too small to provide with social and physical infrastructure - over 80,000 in Zambia for example, over 100,000 in Tanzania - governments resorted to re-settlement schemes to bring villages together in what seemed to be locations of greater economic potential. To spread what were always limited development benefits over the country fairly, they also tended to disperse hospitals, schools, agricultural extension centers in different places, rather than favoring single growth points with a concentration of such service. The conflict between these two policies has been a constant issue in rural development thinking and in national politics throughout East Africa. Re-settlement has worked only where the organizational and material resources of the new enlarged villages matched the demands placed on them by the newly consolidated population. The politically convenient practice of dispersing government financed services has gradually given way to the economically viable practice of concentrating such services in selected growth points with a visible potential for expansion, creating what in effect are rural towns, a developmental transit point on the long march from pastoral to megapolitan Africa.

Self-help as a fashionable theme for development is very attractive to governments facing an immense development problem with very limited resources. By encouraging villages to be self-reliant, vast sums of money could be saved. Governments would help villages that helped themselves. Integrated rural development programs began to be mounted in the mid-seventies to coordinate the work of Ministries of Agriculture with the work of other ministries with spending programs in the rural areas, and a lot of economies arose as a result. Self-help schemes deployed through various routes including rural producer and marketing co-operatives, and they were argued forcibly as a means to avoid the dependency relationships that on a national scale had made African countries so dependent on the industrialized world for technology and supplies. A lot of villages, as we have seen, were already largely self-reliant, but as self-contained communities living at subsistence levels they had little to contribute to the national economy in terms of surplus cash crops, and their production techniques were matched only to this limited and very understandable role. The task for governments was to mobilize their economic potential and make them contribute to the national economy by producing surpluses. To achieve this more was needed than the message of self-help, and the means to achieve rural surpluses have been hotly argued ever since.

The rural development policy options facing East African governments were mainly of two kinds. One offered appropriate technology matched to the absorptive capacity of rural people, with mass distribution of low-cost simplified 'AT' techniques to individual producers whose greater efficiency would then produce the surplus outputs. The other offered advanced, usually highly-mechanized technology for very large production units, usually owned and managed by the state, in which the higher capital cost would be offset by higher yields.

These are not mutually exclusive strategies. Both can be used in parallel, and in East Africa they are. Ethiopia, Zambia, Malawi, Tanzania, Zimbabwe all have large-scale state farms, as well as landed peasantry farming. Objective evaluations are needed to tell which is the most productive, which system is the most efficient in delivering a higher output-to-input ration. Competing sets of data are shown as proof one way or the other all the time. What is clear is that policies that support village self-help through an incrementalist approach using appropriate technology are much more closely matched to village needs and potentials, but are infinitely more difficult to plan and implement. Not only is a detailed knowledge of local circumstances needed to design the increments of technology or infrastructure that are appropriate to a particular village or village type, but also this approach to rural development requires a cadre of villagers able and willing to see the benefits of greater efficiency and output. Neither is readily available to the government official sitting in the East African capital. It does the governments of East African countries great credit that despite these difficulties they have kept alive the policies and programs of supporting self-help in their rural areas. It means they are keeping their ideological options open which is the pragmatic essence of non-alignment in economic management, whatever the slogans say.

The trade-off of output and freedom is, at the present stage of development, implicit in the policy formulations of all East African countries. If the freedoms of rural peoples are severely constrained and if they are subjected to strong dirigiste action by central governments, substantial increases in rural output may be obtained. State organized collectives and co-operatives almost always produce more than villages left to their own devices with no government interventions or support.

If, as an alternative policy, support for self-help is sustained, and efforts are made to understand the productive potential of villages within their own terms, then increases of output can be optimized with the freedom of the rural population to select their own output targets. It is an article of faith to assert that in the long run, output and growth are maximized only if freedom of choice is preserved, so that in the long run, no trade-off is involved. If appropriate technology and finance are delivered carefully, we know that in time villagers are able to undertake their own research and development, and to see and exploit their own potential. Two years of drought and deprivation in East Africa have accentuated this possibility.

That villagers are ready and willing to work for higher yields and rewards is always a parlous matter in rural areas. Traditions die hard. But there is nothing to stop governments from actively instilling ambitions for change among villagers, detonating the cycle of higher output, higher income, and "higher" levels of living and consumption. Rural television centers in Tanzania already do this. In Zambia, the government supports the establishment of rural shops that deliberately tempt villagers to spend more and earn more through higher productivity and the sale of cash crops. That by itself shows an understanding of the balance needed in an economy that is trying to harness the powerful economic effects of self-help.

Economic Development: Comparative Statistics
Selected East African and Other Countries

	(1) Popul. (1982) Total (millions)	(2) km2 % urban	(3) GNP $ 000	(4) GDP per capita (1982)	(5) GDP (1982) $ m	(6) GDP % Agriculture	(7) Industry
Ethiopia	32.9	15	1,222	140	4,010	49	16
Malawi	6.5	10	118	210	1,320	-	-
Uganda	13.5	9	236	230	8,630	82	4
Tanzania	19.8	13	945	280	4,530	52	15
Kenya	18.1	15	583	390	5,340	33	22
Zambia	6.0	45	753	640	3,830	14	36
Zimbabwe	7.5	24	391	850	5,900	15	35
Yemen (YAR)	7.5	14	195	500	3,210	26	17
Saudi Arabia	10.0	69	2,150	16,000	153,590	1	77
United Kingdom	55.8	91	245	9,660	473,220	2	33

Source: World Development Report, 1984 (IBRD/OUP, 1984)

Notes:
(4) calculated by the World Bank Atlas Method
(5-7) converted into $ at the average official exchange rate for 1982
(6) includes farming, forestry, fishing
(7) includes manufacturing, mining, oil, gas, water, electricity, construction

75

Determinant of Income Differentials among Tennessee Counties (1960 and 1970)

by Muhammad Ahmad Al-Saidi,
Vice Chairman, Yemen Free Zones Public Authority

Economic growth, as reflected by a high G.N.P. does not constitute the main objective of development. In recent years, the improvement in the general welfare and equitable income distribution has been realized to be vital in the overall social, political and economic development of a nation.

In spite of greater pressure for social justice and greater equity in the context of rapid economic growth, equitable income distribution has still remained a major problem in almost every country.

Levels of income vary from country to country and from one block of countries to another, while even within a nation there, are income inequalities between different regions. It is these income differentials between regions or sectors which determine the level of development of a country.

Income differentials hinge upon a multitude of social, political, historical, cultural and geographical factors in a country. These factors vary from one country to another.

Issues of Regional Development

There is generally a relatively high degree of factor mobility within a country as compared to factor mobility in the international setting. Factor mobility in conjunction with geographical location and agglomeration of economic activities have important bearing on regional income inequalities.

Initially, regional income differentials tend to increase in the early stages of economic development. Subsequently, factor mobility with increased spread of the processes of economic growth tend to decrease the disparities between regions as the country becomes developed.[1] Furthermore, it has been observed that both skilled and unskilled labor and capital possess greater ability to move from region to region than any other factor of production.

Another major factor effecting regional inequality is the geographic size of the nation, which is positively related to the level of regional inequality. "The larger the geographic size of the national unit, the greater will be the degree of regional inequality."[2]

Regions within nations (due to differences in resource endowment, technology, labor force characteristics) do not possess equal capacity for growth.

Several studies of the United States' economy have focussed on the following factors in order to explain regional economic imbalances: the importance of interregional migration of labor (skilled and unskilled) and capital, regional specialization, interregional linkages, government policy,[3] the stage of economic development, the degree of industrialization, resource endowment, the size, skill, age, sex, of the labor force, and racial barriers.[4]

In this study, attention will be focussed on median family income differential in ninety-five Tennessee counties. Thus the study is an inter-county comparison of median family income differentials and factors determining them. Sources for the data will be the census of 1960, and 1970, and county and city data books.

Counties constitute small units within a particular, relatively small region of the United States. Hence no great diversities in their basic characteristics crop up. The aim of this thesis is to study the county-to-county median family income differentials and not the distribution of median family income within a given county. Even if any two counties have the same median family income, their relative welfare may be different due to differences in the distribution of income within each county.

In view of these considerations, the educational level, the degree of industrialization, the growth rate of employment, imperfections in the labor market and urbanization have been chosen as factors responsible for income differentials among Tennessee counties. To test the importance of these variables as determinants of median family income, a regression model has been formulated, with the hypothesis that the median family income in the county will be higher when:

a) The level of human capital is higher.

b) There is a higher degree of industrialization.
c) The proportion of black population to total is small.
d) The rate of growth of employment is higher.
e) There is greater urbanization.

Theoretical Background and the Model

Voluminous literature is available on income distribution, but there are very few studies which deal with geographical differentials and the factors affecting them.

A study by D. J. Aigner and H. J. Heins entitled "On the Determinant of Income Equality"[5] points out that income is distributed more equitably in regions which have attained a high level of development. It also indicates that the level of income equality is determined by numerous elements related to the process of development.[6] The authors, in their linear regression model, hold social, cultural and political factors constant, in order to determine the changes in the distribution of income.[7] The hypothesis is that income inequality is related to socio-economic factors and level of development stands substantiated by the results of the study. The study further points out the importance of racial barriers in causing increased income inequality in the United States of America, with a statistical significance at the ninety-nine per cent confidence level. The median age of population and median school years completed are also significant at ninety-five per cent and ninety per cent levels respectively.[8]

The authors conclude that, "This is not to suggest that social and economic policies designed to redistribute resources are useless, but, instead, that time and wealth accumulation are on the side of equality. The evidence indicates racial makeup as an important determinant of income inequality is not surprising. And if the distribution of resources is an important aspect of overall social justice, then it would seem that recent public policies designed to remove racial barriers in the social and economic market places of the United States are not misconceived, at least on the basis of their intent."[9]

John W. Foley[10] identifies the determinants of income inequality as follows:

Growth Rate:

"Growth in a social system brings a change in the existing normative order and a diminution of traditional economic relations. Communities experiencing a high rate of in-migration and/or self generated increases in population are expected to have a low degree of inequality. While communities which are remaining stationary or are experiencing a loss in population are expected to have more inequality. Therefore it is hypothesized that the higher the population growth rate the lower the degree of income inequality."[11]

Resource-Level:

Inequality at the national level is related to wealth. The poorer the nation or state, the larger would be the shares of income which accrue to high income groups.[12]

Racial Cleavage:

His study is based on the hypothesis that the higher the percentage of non-white in a community, the higher would be the level of income inequality.[13]

Mature Local Economy:

The percentage of the labor force employed in manufacturing sector is taken as a measure of the maturity of the local economy. "This measure is thought not only to reflect economic maturity but also to directly affect equality, for the higher the per cent employed in manufacturing, the greater the spillover effect of the usually superior wages paid in this sector to other sectors of the local economy.[14]

Thus a mature and developed economy will have a lower level of income inequality.

Population Density:

"Accompanying an increase in population density is a more heterogeneous and differentiated social structure which results in more competition in the work force. Also, urban areas would seem to be a center of capital formation which predict inequality. Accordingly it is hypothesized that the greater the number of people per square mile, the greater the income equality."[15]

Family Participation in the Work Force:

"The total number of members of family in the work force would tend to lower difference in income between families for the lower the income of the primary wages earner, the greater the incentive for participation in the work force by members of the family."16 The most desirable indicator of the extent of family participation in the labor force would be the mean number of members working. Since this was not available, the female percentage of work force was employed as an alternative. It is assumed that the higher the rate of female participation in the work force the lower the rate of income inequality."[16]

Agribusiness Activity:

"It is thought that the more a county depends upon agriculture for its economy, the more the disparity between family incomes. The preferable measure of agribusiness activity would be the per cent of the work force employed in agriculture. But, such a measure would have introduced multicollinearity into the model because the per cent of the work force employed in agriculture is highly related in a negative manner to the percentage of the work force employed in manufacturing. The indicator that was related to the dependent variable is the per cent of land in the community devoted to agriculture."[17]

After estimating the model by multiple regression, the results reveal a negative relationship between the community's economy, the level of material resources and the growth rate to income inequality. He also found a positive relationship between racial cleavage and population density to income inequality.[18]

The author also examined the implications of public policy and its effects on income inequality and found a positive weak relationship between the level of income inequality and public spending. But there were strong positive relationships between the degree of inequality and the level of public policy outputs in the SMSA[19] counties where inequality was highest and most visible.[20]

Although the study undertaken deals with income level, not income distribution, of the counties, it is thought to be useful to present Foley's principal findings from his study of United States counties. The assumption that imperfections in the labor market, which are due to racial discrimination, will decrease in relation to the rate of development of the community and the hypothesis that growth in the rate of employment depends upon a relative increase in education, are substantiated by Foley's findings that income inequalities diminish in proportion to the level of development attained and that an increase in the percentage of the non-white population of a community proportionately widens income disparities.

Williamson's[21] international cross-section analysis and study of the United States found that the regional income differentials bear a positive relationship to development. The author mentions the following factors to be responsible for the income differential:

Labor Migration:

The out-flow of the more skilled and educated labor from the poor regions in the early stages of development diminishes the growth possibilities of the relatively poor regions (south). There will be an extra burden for those who stay in the poor region (south) as a result of a fall in the labor participation rate in that region which means an increase in the participation rate in the more developed region. This burden will increase with a rise in the rate of out-migration.[22]

Williamson observes that as economic development proceeds, the poor region will begin to develop, the high costs of migration will diminish and occupational wage differences between the two regions are also likely to diminish. Thus there will be a change in the composition of the internal migration. Specifically, he suggests, that after the World War II[23] the southern United States region not only retained its educated and skilled labor, but may have even attracted the educated labor from the developed regions in the north.

Capital Migration:

A scarcity of capital in the poor region does not always imply high marginal productivity and high rental prices which would attract more capital. Capital flows are heavily influenced by growth rate. In early stages of development such factors as external economies and general benefits derived from agglomeration of capital projects in the north, lack of entrepreneurial ability, and the non-existence of developed capital markets in the south caused the out-migration of capital from the south to the north.

However, there may be further national development which causes a reversal of the previous situation with capital flowing from the north to the south, or at least the outflow from the south will tend to stop. That is because an improvement in the national capital market, the benefits from external economics, and the agglomeration of capital may become exhausted in the north, and may begin to appear in the south.

Interregional Linkages:

Williamson also believes that there may be a lack of interregional linkages in the early stages of national growth so that the spread effects of technological change, social change, and income multipliers are minimized. Part of the national growth process is simply economic unification of regional markets. To the extent that such interregional linkages are slow in developing national economic growth is all the more likely to be regionalized in the, earliest stages of growth. However, in the later stages of national development there will be an increase in the interregional linkages due to improvements in transportation, communications and the creation of national markets. These factors will tend to reverse the regional differences of income.[24]

Central Government Policy:

In the early stages of development, when available resources are scarce, there will be a tendency in the federal government toward allocating investment in the north where "urgent demands for several types of capital intensive public investment appear.[25] This favors the fast-growing industrial regions and helps generate even more rapid growth causing increased requirements for social overhead capital in the future.

Subsequently in late stages, as the problem of regional inequality increases and the social tension becomes acute, the federal government has to change its policies.

In his study, Williamson asserts that "any of the previous factors, or any combination of them, may be enough to cause regional inequality to diminish. once the process of regional convergence or depolarization begins, however it is likely to become cumulative, with the forces tending towards regional equality mutually strengthening each other and contributing to a more rapid speed of adjustment."[26]

The Empirical Results

The regression equation with median family income as dependent variable and five independent variables is estimated. The data for 1960 and 1970, which is employed in the cross-section analysis pertains to ninety-five Tennessee counties. Using the statistics, four variables are significantly associated with the dependent variable (median family income) at the 99 and/or 95 percent level. These variables are: the percent of the population, urban, the degree of industrialization, the level of education, and the percent of population that is nonwhite.

Without going into the details of the mathematical calculations, the results are summarized as follows:

As we predicted above, the results demonstrate the importance of education as a determinant of median family income in Tennessee counties. Thus, as the level of education increases by one year, the median family income will increase by $199.90, ceteris paribus.

The degree of industrialization is positively correlated with median family income. So, the median family income will increase by $24.30 as a result of one per cent increase in the degree of industrialization. Its t-value is highly significant even at 0.0005 level.

Race composition has a negative correlation with the median family income which implies that the median family income will decrease by $8.3 as a result of an increase in the race composition by one per cent, ceteris paribus.

Finally, urbanization is positively correlated with the median family income in Tennessee counties. Thus, if urbanization increases by one per cent the median family income will increase by $20.60 in the county ceteris paribus.

The above analysis was repeated for 1970 using the variables previously described. Only four variables are significantly associated with the median family income. The variables are: The education level, degree of industrialization, rate of growth of employment, and per cent of population living in an urban area. Race composition was not significant; therefore, it has been excluded.

The interpretation of this result is, other effects remaining constant, median family income will increase: $441.70 as a result of an increase in the level of education by one year, by $67.10 as the degree of industrialization increased by one per cent, by $10.20 in response to a one per cent increase in the rate of growth of employment, and by $12.60 in response to a one per cent increase in the urbanization.

However, some differences may be noted in the relative importance of several of the explanatory variables between 1960-1970.

1. The improvement in the level of education is largely responsible for the inter-county variation in median family income in 1970 as against that of 1960. The marginal productivity of labor in 1970 was approximately twice as much as it was a decade earlier. The accelerating pace of technological development in a modern economy requires highly skilled and trained people in order to have the economy functioning productively. The need for highly educated and technically competent persons increases with the technological strides made by a nation. It is evident that the productivity of labor increases with the improvement in education. However, it may be noted in passing that in underdeveloped economies where agriculture is traditional with regard to both crops grown and farming practices, education may have little effect on productivity.[27]

2. The association between the degree of industrialization and median family income was positive in 1960 and 1970. This result is not surprising because of the well-known disequilibria and income differentials between agriculture and the non-agricultural sectors. Moreover, workers in the non-agricultural sector embody more human capital. Thus, the degree of industrialization determines the rate of productivity as well as the level of income within the county. As is evident from the regression equation, the

effect of industrialization in 1970 was higher in comparison to the previous years.
3. The rate of growth of employment in the preceding decade has a positive correlation with the median family income in Tennessee counties, but it was significant only in 1970. It is not clear why such disparate results were obtained.
4. Race composition had a negative correlation with the median family income in Tennessee counties, but it was significant only in 1960. As societies become more developed the level of discrimination decreases and as the blacks become qualified for better jobs the importance of race composition as a variable that negatively explains the income differential, diminishes. Perhaps more important, the U.S. government has the last twenty years made discrimination illegal and prompted programs favoring minorities. A more important feature concerning the population of Tennessee is that the majority of the black community resides in west Tennessee while most of the white population lives in the eastern part which is relatively poor. Relatively faster increases in the income of the western region during the period 1960-1970 are probably in part responsible for the 1970 results.
5. As shown by the two censuses, urbanization has a positive correlation with median family income although it was less significant in 1970 than in the previous years, probably because of the green revolution in the agricultural sector.

Conclusion

The above empirical results support the current theory explaining the pattern of regional inequality. We find this result despite the similarity in characteristics that may exist in the units of study (counties) of the present thesis.

There is no doubt that the education level, degree of industrialization, race composition, urbanization, and rate of growth of employment, were the major factors determining the regional inequalities in Tennessee. The western region of Tennessee and the western part of midTennessee were found to have, in general, a higher rate of growth than the eastern region, using the model estimated in this study.

Issues of Regional Development

1. Jeffrey G. Williamson, "Regional Inequality and the Process of National Development," Economic Development and Cultural Change, XIII (July 1965): 4-8.
2. Ibid., p. 20.
3. For further detail see: Ibid., pp. 4-8 and Forest G. Hill, "Regional Aspects of Economic Development," Land Economics, XXXVIII (May 1960): 87.
4. See: Ali-samarrie and Miller, "State Differentials in Income Concentration," American Economic Review (March 1967): 59-72 and Aigner, Heins, "On the Determination of Income Equality," American Economic Review (March 1967) 175-184.
5. D.J. Aigner and A. J. Heins, "On the Determinants of Income Equality," The American Economic Review 57, (March 1967): 175-183.
6. Ibid., p. 175.
7. Ibid., p. 176.
8. Ibid., p. 178.
9. Ibid., pp. 180-81.
10. J. W. Foley, "Trends, Determinants and Policy Implication of Income Inequality in United States Counties," Social and Soc. Res. 61 (Jl' 1977): 441-61.
11. Ibid., p. 445.
12. Ibid., pp. 445-46.
13. Ibid., p. 446.
14. Ibid., p. 446.
15. Ibid., p. 447.
16. Ibid., p. 447.
17. Ibid., pp. 447-57.
18. Ibid., pp. 456-57.
19. (SMSA): Standard Metropolitan Statistical Areas.
20. Ibid., p. 457.
21. Jeffrey G. Williamson, "Regional Inequality and the Process of National Development," "Economic Development and Cultural Change, XIII (July 1965): 3.
22. Ibid., pp. 4-6.
23. Ibid., p. 8.
24. Ibid., pp. 7-8.
25. Ibid., p. 7.
26. Ibid., p 9.
27. Anthony M. Tanig, "Economic Development and Changing Consequences of Race Discrimination in Southern Agriculture" Journal of Farm Economics Vol. 41, (Dec.1950): p. 1115.

Bibliography

Aigner, D. J. and Heins, A. J., "On the Determinants of Income Equality," American Economic Review 57, No. 1. (March 1967): 175-184.

Al-samarie, A. and Miller, "State Differentials in Income Concentration," American Economic Review 57, No. 1 (March 1967): 59-72.

Foley, J. W., "Trends, Determinants and Policy Implications."

Greenhut, M. L., "Needed—A Return to the Classics in Regional Economic Development Theory," Kyklos XIX (May 1966): 472.

Hill, Forest G., "Regional Aspects of Economic Development," Land Economics, XXXVIII, No. 2 (May 1962): 85-98.

Isard, Walter, and Cumberland, J. H. Regional Economic Planning. Paris: O.E.C.C., 1961.

Kelejian, Harry H. and Oates, Wallace E. Introduction to Econometrics. New York: Harper & Row, Inc., 1974. Mason, Robert D. Statistical Techniques in Business and Economics. Homewood: Richard D. Irwin, Inc.,

Meyer, J. R., "Regional Economics: A Survey, "American Economic Review, LIII (March 1963): 1954.

Mills, Frederick C. Statistical Methods. New York: Henry Holt and Company, 1955.

Richardson, H.W. Regional Economics. London: MacMillan, and Aldine Publishing Company, 1968.

Tang, Anthony M., "Economic Development and Changing Consequences of Race Discrimination in Southern Agriculture," Journal of Farm Economics 41 (Dec. 1959): 1113-1126

U.S. Department of Commerce. Bureau of the Census. United States Census of Population: 1970. Vol. 1, Characteristics of the Population, pt. 44, Tennessee.

— County and City Data Book (A Statistical Abstract Supplement): 1977.

— County and City Data Book (A Statistical Abstract Supplement): 1967.

— County and City Data Book: 1962.

— United States Census of Population: 1960. Vol. 1, Characteristics of Population, pt. 44, Tennessee.

— County and City Data Book: 1960.

— County and City Data Book: 1952.

Williamson, J. G., "Regional Inequality and the Process of National Development: A description of Patterns," Economic Development and Cultural Change, XIII, No. 4, pt. 11 (July 1965): 3-84.

The Role of Education in Developing Japan

by Professor Toshio Toyoda, International College of Commerce and Economy in Tokyo

The technological advances achieved in Japan should be considered as a result of the extensive efforts made by the Japanese industry. It is also necessary to note that factors such as economic, social and government policies, responding to international circumstances, have made important contributions as well. However, the most crucial element responsible for the advances in technology is Japan's high level of education, which had been fostered long ago, beginning in earlier centuries.

International circumstances were so favorable at the beginning of the so-called "take-off period" that Japan could launch herself into the ocean of modernization without receiving any foreign assistance in that stage.

The aim of this paper is to consider the role of Japan's education in the context of self-help development. We will fail to comprehend the economic advances of Japan unless we consider the educational endeavors.

Early Beginnings of Education in Japan

Many scholars in Europe and the United States highly evaluate the role that education has played in the modernization of Japan. Professor E.O. Reischauer states: "When, in the 19th century, Japan withstood the challenge of Europe and the United States, which boasted of superiority as the leaders of the world economy, this was the result of Japan's high learning ratio and splendid educational level. Answering the questions of what lies at the core of the Japanese society and what has contributed to Japan's success, nothing has been more important than education."

R.P. Dore and H. Passin claim that the groundwork and foundation of Japan's modern educational system were completed in the Tokugawa Period[1] and, in that sense, modernization from the Meiji Era[2] onward owes much to the legacy of Tokugawa.

Dore states that Japan was one of the few countries aside from those of Western Europe able to maintain their independence and to advance industrially. Dore links this with the spread of education prior to the Meiji Era. He points out that in the latter part of the Edo Period[3], 45% of the men and 15% of the women were attending some kind of school, (private elementary "terakoya" (temple) school, or private "juku" (clan) school). Accordingly, it is believed that the Japanese of this era had considerable reading and writing ability, and that there was a high literacy rate. This compares very favorably with the advanced countries of the mid-19th century (on par with men in Italy and with women in France).

The spread of "terakoya" education contributed to the development of a modern society after the Meiji Restoration. It aroused a popular desire to absorb Western civilization. Meanwhile, progressive teachers aided the birth of a new educational system based on the French system in 1872, just five years after the Meiji Restoration.

Education for Industrial Development and its Problems

During the early part of the Meiji Era, those engaged in primary industries centering on agriculture, accounted for more than 80% of the entire population. Light industries centering on spinning, were established around the time between the Sino-Japanese War (1894-95) and the Russo-Japanese War (1904-05). Even when compulsory education was extended to six years in 1907, the percentage of school attendance remained at an almost equal level.

Secondary education gradually expanded, too. The rate of pupils continuing from primary education to secondary education rose from 4.3% in 1895 to 15% in 1920 and then to 25% in 1940. Looking at this increase on a regional level, it will be discovered that it corresponds exactly to the development of industrialization. Major expansion happened in Tokyo and Osaka, accompanied by minor ones in Kochi and Miyazaki. Although the pace of development of higher education was finally accelerated after World War I, only some 2.5% of the Japanese youth were receiving education beyond the secondary level at that time.

It was only after 1960 that the quantitative expansion of higher education showed conspicuous progress. By 1970, the rate of pupils continuing with university education exceeded 30%. A "well-educated society" appeared. However, as a consequence, the elite position of university graduates vanished. Many were crowded out of managerial and specialized jobs into clerical and sales jobs, formerly held by secondary education graduates.

It is also necessary to point out the limitations and drawbacks of pre-war education. Among the "hired foreign teachers" invited by the government during the Meiji Period, there were some who even at that time criticized obsolete and unscientific aspects of the curriculum. There were others who could perceive a taint of class consciousness in the "double track system" of Japanese education. Still others criticized the ultra-nationalism which pervaded teaching ethics.

None of these criticisms were entirely erroneous, but it must be born in mind that at that time Japan was primarily concerned with catching up with the advanced countries as rapidly as possible. Education advanced under the slogans of "civilization and enlightenment", "growth of industry and production", "wealth and military strength", and "Japanese spirit and Western learning". The imitation of Western European culture was applied to a large extent, yet excluding the rational, critical, and individualistic spirit forming the basis of Western European civilization. While the foreign teachers fully recognized the great enthusiasm and quality of Japanese students, they could not ignore the deficiencies of the Japanese education.

Historical Review of the Spread of Education in Japan

The development of education in Japan may be said to resemble that of the United States, considering the fact that elementary education was almost completely universal within a short period of 30 to 40 years after its introduction to Japan. It was followed by a very rapid development of secondary education. Higher education also has developed rapidly in recent years, following the expansion of secondary education. Except for the spread of education for women which has been comparatively slow, it can be said that education in Japan, as in the United States and the U.S.S.R. is characterized by a rapid rate of development and widespread popularization.

In the beginning of the Meiji Era, when the modernization of Japan began, the modern educational system was created. Elementary education, offering fundamental education to all people, and higher education for the purpose of training the leadership were first developed and pushed forward the modernization of the Japanese society and economy. The educational system was expanded during the following years, during which a national economy was developed on the basis of light industries, chiefly spinning. At the same time, the foundation for a heavy industry was laid. As the result of the spread of elementary education, secondary education was promoted as well, together with the development of vocational and women's education. When heavy industries developed further and the Japanese economy reached a high level of maturity, the educational system was further expanded, and higher education was developed following the spread of secondary education.

The Meiji government, which started the modernization of Japan later than the Western countries, endeavored to secure her independence and to develop the country towards the level already achieved by the more advanced countries. Modern production methods were introduced, while at the same time modern military, administrational, and financial institutions were established. Slogans were created, such as "Enrich the country and strengthen its arms", "Increase products and promote industries", and "Civilize the country and enlighten the people".

The establishment of a national educational system was one of the objectives of such policies. In 1872, the 5th year of Meiji, following the educational system of the West, the Government Order of Education was promulgated based on the modern idea of equal opportunity for education. This heralded the dawn of modern education in Japan.

The modernization of Japan was accelerated by governmental actions, such as abolishing the feudal caste system and establishing a modern national educational system for developing industries and increasing production.

Even in the Tokugawa Era, temple schools and other private schools enjoyed considerable popular support. Efforts by the government to establish a modern educational system were favored by the people. As a result, the percentage of elementary school attendance rose from only 28% in 1873 to over 50% as early as 1883, and has exceeded 96% since 1906.

At the elementary level, the full enforcement of four years of compulsory education was completed in 1900. In 1908, it was extended to cover six years.

In 1893, laws concerning complementary vocational schools as an institution of semi-secondary education were promulgated. And in 1899, laws were passed concerning vocational schools and high schools for girls as institutions of general secondary education. Vocational education and women's education were thus established.

After 1895, the percentage of elementary school enrollment has gradually decreased while that of secondary and higher education has increased.

From about 1893 to 1899, various kinds of secondary and semi-secondary educational institutions, including high schools for girls, vocational schools, and complementary vocational schools, were established in addition to middle schools. This was during the period between the Sino-Japanese and Russo-Japanese wars. The Japanese economy was just entering a stage of early development. The seeds of modern industry sown in the early Meiji Era had grown. Cottage industry began to be reorganized into factory industry, such as the transition from hand-weaving to mechanical spinning. The educational function fulfilled by the traditional apprenticeship was now taken over by the new vocational schools. Socioeconomic needs began to be satisfied by the public educational system.

Secondary education, which began to develop since the time of the Sino-Japanese War (1894/95), experienced a rapid growth when the Japanese economy reached a level of maturity during the period from the end of the Meiji Era to the Showa Era.

The Role of Vocational Education and Training

Japan's modern educational system originated in 1872, the 5th year of the Meiji Era. Around 1900, the vocational education was improved and systematized. This amounted to a reform of the educational system in anticipation of the industrial revolution which made swift progress in those years. The government believed that the "people's vocational knowledge and skill" constituted an invaluable capital for enriching and strengthening the nation. Thus it began to create lower institutions of vocational education, such as vocational supplementary schools, apprentice schools, and simplified agricultural schools.

In 1893, laws concerning complementary vocational schools as an institution of semi-secondary education, and in 1899, laws for vocational schools were promulgated.

The development of enrollment in vocational courses on the level of secondary education can be considered an indication of Socioeconomic change. A comparison of enrollment in general courses and in vocational courses of secondary schools shows that the former had decreased from 84% in 1895 to 67% in 1920, and to 58% in 1960.

All courses were so closely related to the Socioeconomic developments that each one has been changing constantly, responding to the various requirements of industry. The population employed in secondary industry started from the lowest percentage and increased continuously each decade until 1960. The population of the tertiary industry showed a very similar trend, except during the early 50ies.

The main characteristics of Japan's vocational education and training can be summarized in the following paragraphs:

Socio-cultural circumstances prior to the development of education were favorable because Japan was a single state, had no colonial past and a highly literate population.

Financial assistance from the government outlined in the national subsidy law (1894), and self-reliance of local communities guaranteed rapid development. 50%, i.e. half of the educational expenses, were borne by the local community.

Loose regulations in vocational schools resulted in varying length of schooling and in some schools accepting pupils who had not finished elementary education.

The head master of an apprentice school was appointed by the government and paid highly. The instructor of the school was chosen among the Shokunin, the artisans, who had the highest level of skill. All imported textbooks were translated into Japanese within one decade.

Each apprentice school had supplementary courses on the elementary level, avoiding impractical theory.

The status of vocational schools was considered lower than that of general schools. The rate of drop-outs was high, because parents wanted their children to help them at home.

Along with the industrial development, the social demand for vocational schools increased. Many apprentice schools were upgraded to upper ordinary secondary schools.

Technological Innovation and Higher Education in Engineering

One of the most important factors affecting the technological development are studies and researches undertaken in engineering. Education in engineering has played a major role in the expansion of technological development in the last few decades.

The industrial world was in high demand of technological manpower after the war. To meet this request, the Japanese government decided to establish a new type of university. At that time, there were only 7 universities which aimed at training and bringing up a small elite in science and technology. In 1949, 180 new universities were opened almost simultaneously.

Education in engineering was adapted to the demands of the technological boom. The universities, new and old, tried to adapt by revising not only their curriculum and courses, but also by introducing new types of laboratories and new faculties. Without the expansion of education in engineering, we could not have expected the subsequent development in such industries as ship-building, iron and steel, oil and chemicals, electronics, and so on.

Another important point is the so-called "on-the-job training". This might sometimes be overlooked, but in Japan, the role played by on-the-job training was, and is fairly important. It provides new skills and knowledge to staff in a system of life-long employment.

In the history of modernization, Japan's challenge of development has been to catch up with the Western civilization. In one century, she has fortunately achieved a high level of industrialization. The most important task for Japan today is to make contributions in innovative technology. Academic and business circles discuss this subject very often. The rather weak post graduate education may be one of the reasons why Japan still lags behind in this regard.

The following ratio clearly shows Japan's weak points with regard to higher education in science and technology. The ratio of attendance after the age of 22 years is only 1.2% of one age group, while it is 16.3% in the USA, 13.2% in Germany, and 9.6% in France.

We come to the conclusion that basic education (primary and secondary) played a significant role in the prewar and postwar industrial development of Japan. Higher education came later and gradually contributed to the technological expansion. Therefore, substantial innovative findings can be expected in the coming decade, as fruits of the post-graduate education in engineering.

Japan's Development and Human Resources

Japan has become recognized by the world today as a major power in economy and trade. Many people recognize also that this was made possible by the high standard of education in Japan.

This high educational standard and the Japanese people's enthusiasm for education are further confirmed by a survey investigating the percentage of private

Further Suggested Readings and Bibliography of English Language Books on Education

1. Ministry of Education: "Japan's Growth and Education". 1963.
2. Ronald P. Dore: "Education in Tokugawa Japan". 1965.
3. Herbert Passin: "Society and Education in Japan". 1965.
4. Michio Nagai: "Higher Education In Japan - Its Take-off and Crash". 1971.
5. Ministry of Foreign Affairs: "Education and Japan's Modernization". 1972.
6. OECD: "Japan - Reviews of National Policies for Education". 1971.
7. Ronald P. Dore: "The Diploma Disease - Education, Qualification, and Development". 1976.
8. Edwin O. Reischauer: "The Japanese". 1979.
9. Ezla Vogel: "Japan as Number One". 1979.
10. Bibliographies:
    Herbert Passin: "Japanese Education: "A Bibliography of Materials in the English Language". 1970.
    Teichler Ulrich, and Friedrich Voss: "Bibliography on Japanese Education: Postwar Publications in Western Languages". 1974.

---

[1] Tokugawa: Japanese Shogun dynastie founded by Tokugawa Ieyasu, who was given the title of "Shogun" by the Emperor (Tenno) in 1603. The 15th and last Shogun of this dynastie handed government back to the Tenno in 1868.

[2] Meiji (Japanese: "enlighted government") was the government policy of Emperor Mutsuhito, also called "Meiji Tenno", who, in 1868, ended the Shogunate and reestablished the political power of the Tenno. In the Meiji era, the strict seclusion of Japan from the outside world (enforced from 1637) was lifted, and the building of a modem nation according to the European model began.

[3] Edo (or Yedo) was the old name of Tokyo till 1868. Edo was the seat of the Tokugawa Shoguns. After the breakdown of the Shogunate, the Emperor moved his government seat to Tokyo from the ancient capital Kyoto.

Contributors

Dirar Abduldaim, a Yemeni national, is an engineer by profession. He is currently working as Director General for the Computing Systems at the Ministry of Local Administration. His past work experience includes an assignment as Director General for Public Relations at the same ministry, and Chief Engineer for CYDA. He completed a study in Laser Technology at the Institute for Theoretic Physics, Triest, Italy in 1988. In 1982, he did a course on Alternative Energy at the Florida University in the USA. Earlier, in 1975, he obtained a certificate from the Bou Center for International Education, Rotterdam, Holland, in the field of low cost housing. He received his original master degree in Building Technologies from the Moscow Academy of Engineering in 1971. He has published numerous articles in Yemeni magazines and newspapers, as well as in "Asia and Africa Today" of the former Soviet Union.

Eberhart Lutz, a German national, is currently working with the German Bank, branch office in Geneva, Switzerland. His field of specialization is giving advice on potential investments in the Middle East. His work experience includes an assignment by the German Technical Aid (GTZ) as a social worker for the Yemeni-German Harraz Afforestation Project. Earlier, he was working as an Arabic language tutor with the German Development Service (DED). He holds an MA degree in Islamic Sciences from the Free University of Berlin. Among his publications are: "Die Local Development Associations der Jemenitischen Arabischen Republik", in "Orient" Periodical, Hamburg 1983; and "Arabia Felix. Ein Reisebericht aus dem Nordjemen", Kerbe Verlag, Berlin.

Fritz Piepenburg, a German national, is currently working as a consultant to the German Technical Aid (GTZ) in Sana'a, and as correspondent for the Middle East Times. He has been living in Yemen since 1975. Between 1980 and 1984, he studied Arabic Literature and Islamic History at the Sana'a University. He is also acting as Secretary General of the Professors World Peace Academy in Yemen. Among his publications are "New Traveller's Guide to Yemen", Sana'a 1987; "Sana'a Al-Qadeema: The Challenges of Modernization" in "The Middle East City", New York 1987; and "Sechs Lieder aus dem Jemen" in "Jemen - 3000 Jahre Kunst und Kultur des Glücklichen Arabien", Frankfurt 1987.

Vivian Craddock Williams, a British national, is an economist by profession. He has been working as an economic advisor to the Industrial Bank of Yemen. His previous assignments include Kenya, Tanzania, and other East African countries. He has written numerous contributions to periodicals and magazines specialized in economic issues.

Dr. Muhammad Ahmad Al-Saidi, a Yemeni national, holds the position of Vice Chairman to the Yemen Free Zones Authority. His previous assignments include Chairman of the Yemen Oil and Minerals Corporation, Secretary General of the Supreme Council for Oil and Mineral Resources, Director General of the Geological Survey, Minerals and Petroleum Authority, and Undersecretary for Industry at the Ministry of Economy and Industry. He holds an MA in Economics and a Ph.D. in Industrial Economy with First Class Honors. He has published several books, like "The Development of a Consumer Society: The Case of Yemen" (1985); "Industrial Strategies for Yemen" (1990); and "Determinant of Industrial Development in Yemen" (1990).

Prof. Toshio Toyoda, a Japanese national, is a Professor of Educational Sociology at the Tokyo International University. Pervious assignments include Professor of Social Engineering at the University of Tsukuba, Visiting Fellow to the Institute for Development Studies at the University of Sussex, and Visiting Professor to the University of Nairobi. He graduated from the Faculty of Literature at the University of Tohoku, and finished the graduate course in the Faculty of Education at the University of Tokyo. His publications include "The Role of Education in Japan's Industrialization" in "Look Japan" Magazine, 1983; "Japan in its Take-Off Period", University of Tokyo, 1982; "From Apprentice to Worker - Vocational Training and Industrialization", UN Japan, 1982; and "Education in Asia", 1978.

List of Abbreviations

AB	Administrative Board (of LCCD)
CC	Coordination Council
CCD	Committee for Civil Defence
CLCCD	Confederation of Local Councils for Cooperative Development
CoM	Council of Ministers
CPO	Central Planning Organization
CYDA	Confederation of Yemeni Development Associations
EC	Executive Council
GA	General Assembly (of LCCD)
GDP	Gross Domestic Product
GNP	Gross National Product
GSLCCD	General Secretariat for the Local Councils for Cooperative Development
LC	Local Council
LCCD	Local Council for Cooperative Development
LDA	Local Development Association
ME	Middle East
MoLA	Ministry of Local Administration
PDRY	People's Democratic Republic of Yemen
PGC	People's General Congress
PLC	People's Local Council
PWPA	Professors World Peace Academy
RoY	Republic of Yemen
SMSA	Standard Metropolitan Statistical Areas
YAR	Yemen Arab Republic
YD	Yemen Dinar
YES	Yemen Economic Society
YR	Yemen Rial
YSP	Yemen Socialist Party

Photographic Impressions of the Seminar

The opening session on May 13, 1985. Sitting at the head table from left to right: Dr. Muhammad Ahmad Al-Saidi, Undersecretary of Economics; Dr. Abdulaziz Saqqaf, Professor of Economics at the Sanaa University; Dr. Ahmad Al-Asbahi, Minister of Labor and Social Affairs; Muhammad Al-Shuhati, Chairman of the Agricultural and Cooperative Credit Bank.

Presentations and round-table talks during the following day.

Prof. Toshio Toyoda explains the role of education in developing Japan.

انخفضت الى حد كبير في السبعينات.

وفي الفصل الاخير (توشيو تويودا، دور التعليم في التنمية اليابانية) توضيح « المعجزة الاقتصادية» لدولة اليابان. البرفسور توتودا يؤكد وبشدة على أهمية الدور الذي يلعبه التعليم. والاقتصاد القومي حيث ان اليابان لديها تقاليد قديمة وعريقة خاصه بالتعليم تعود جذورها الى قرون ماضيه. ولقد كان التعليم الاجباري لفترة اربع سنوات من الاشياء التي أرسيت وترسخت دعائمها في بداية القرن التاسع عشر للميلاد وكان الحضور يفوق ٩٦ في المئة في عام ١٩٠٦م. وفي نفس الوقت تحسن مستوى التعليم المهني مع كامل التنسيق لمتطلبات الصناعة وكانت نصف المصاريف المدرسية التعليمية تدفع بواسطة المجتمعات المحلية وعلى وجه التحديد الاباء.. وكان كثير من الاهتمام مركز على رعاية وتحسين هيئات تدريس للجامعات وخاصه للفروع الهندسية مع التعاون والتنسيق المتقارب لمتطلبات الصناعة والتطوير. ومن عادات اليابانيين انهم يعيشوا في بيوت صغيره ولكن الاباء دائماً مستعدون للتضحية والعيش في مساحة صغيره حتى يعطوا لابنائهم مساحة خاصه للمذاكرة والاستذكار. ولقد أكدت احصائية أجريت في اليابان عام ١٩٧٩م على أن ٧٦ في المئة من تلاميذ المدارس الابتدائيه لديهم غرفهم الخاصة للمذاكرة وهذا المعدل اكثر بكثير من دول أخرى حتى في الدول الغربية الصناعية المتقدمة.

١ ينطلق المتحمسون لفكرة الحلقة المفرغة للفقر من ان كل مجتمع متخلف يقع في مجموعة دائرية من العوامل التي يتأثر ويؤثر الواحد منها في الآخر على نحو من شأنه الابقاء على المستوى الاقتصادي والاجتماعي بالبلاد الفقيرة على ما هو عليه.

٢ تنطلق في هذا الاستنتاج من ان الدخل الذي سيولد في المناطق الريفيه سيوزع بشكل اكثر عداله ونفعاً على فئات من المجتمع معدنية الدخل وبالتالي تقل احتمالات تهريب جزء كبير منه الى الخارج وسينصب معظمه الى قنوات الطلب كما ان نوعية الطلب في هذه الحاله تختلف عنها في المدن حيث يتجه المستهلك الريفي ذو الدخل المنخفض بسبب عنه في المدينه، سيتجه الى استهلاك السلع الضروريه والتي اغلبها تنتجة محلياً، بدلاً من الاتجاه نحو استهلاك الكماليات المستورده؟ وهو امر يؤدي الى زيادة الحافز للاستثمار وتخفيف الضغط على رصيد النقد الاجنبي بتخفيض الاستيراد.

١٠

الحكومه مرتباتهم. وبالرغم من كل هذه المعوقات الخطيره والتي تقرض في كيان البنيه الاساسيه لفكرة الاعتماد على النفس لازالت المجالس المحليه للتطوير التعاوني قادرة على انجاز نتائج ملموسه وجديره بالذكر على مدى السنوات الاخيره.

الجزء الثاني من الكتاب يعالج قضايا تطوير المناطق في ثلاثة دول مختلفه وهي : تنزانيا، والتي تمثل أفريقيا والعالم الثالث بشكل عام وتنيسي أحدى ولايات الولايات المتحده الامريكيه والتي تمثل التطور في العالم الصناعي الغربي ذو اليابان والتي تمثل العملاق الاقتصادي الصاعد من حيث التطور والمكونات لبروز قوة جديده في القرن الواحد والعشرين. وكل هذه الابحاث الثلاثة تشير الى أهمية التعليم كأهم الضمانات لإنجاح عمليات التطوير المحليه.

وفي الفصل الرابع (**فيقيان كرادوك ويلميز، الاقتصادات الغير منحازة لقري شرق أفريقيا**) والباحث شخصية ذات خبرة طويله في شئون شرق أفريقيا وعلى وجه الخصوص دولة تنزانيا. يرى الباحث بأن الامكانيات الزراعيه في اليمن ليست مستغلة تماماً لان حوالي اكثر من ٨٠ في المئة من اجمالي السكان يعيشون خارج المدن وبالرغم من هذا الزراعه والتصنيـــع الريفي تساهم بأقل م ٢٦ في المئة من منتوجات الدخل القومي. ان احد نماذج القرى في شرق أفريقيا حسب تقدير ويليمز تعتبر من التكوينات المعزوله ولهذا فإنها تكوين طبيعي نما خلال هذه القرون معتمداً على نفسه وليس على واضعي النظريات. وبالرغم من هذا تدخل الحكومة في بعض الحالات لزيادة الانتاج القومي. الكاتب ويليمز يعطي بعض الفضل لدول شرق أفريقيا في محافظتهم وابقائهم على برامج التعاونيات ودعمهم لفكرة الاعتماد على النفس بطريقة عمليه واقعيه. والحكومه من جانب آخر تدعم المؤسسات التي تحث على الاعتماد على النفس ولكن تترك لهم المجال لتنفيذ هذا العمل بأنفسهم. والكاتب ويليمز يعتقد بأنه عندما تعمل محلا من دوائر الانتاج المرتفـع والدخل المرتفع والمستوى المرتفع، التقدم في مجال التنميه سوف يتصاعد فوراً.

وفي الفصل الخامس (**د. محمد احمد السعيدي، محددات الدخل في مقاطعات ولاية تنيسي بالولايات الأمريكية المتحدة**) قام بدراسة العوامل التي تتحكم في دخل الاسره لاكثر من ٩٥ مقاطعه في ولاية تنيسي لعام ١٩٦٠م. حيث توصل الباحث الى بعض الاستنتاجات المهمه التي حصل عليها بواسطة توظيف الطرق التحليليه الرياضية وتوصل السعيدي الى أن مستوى التعليم هو المحدد الرئيسي للدخل. وتاتي بعد هذا العامل عوامل اخرى مثل درجة التصنيـع، والتمييز العرقي، ومدى التمدن او التحضر، ومعدل نمو اليد العامله. هذا ولقد كان للتمييز العرقي اثر سلبي على الدخل في الستينات إلا ان اهمية النسبة

الخطه الخمسية الأولى كانت عظيمه ولقد ضمنت هذه الخطه النجاح للتعاون بين الهيئات التعاونية المحليه والحكومه.

والفصل الثاني (ابرهارد لوتز، الهيئات التعاونية الأهلية وأثارها الاجتماعية والسياسية) سلط بعض الضوء على التطوير قبل عام ١٩٧٣م وظهور ظاهرة المؤسسات للتعاونيات ما بين عامي ١٩٧٣م وعام ١٩٧٥م. وعند التدقيق في دراسة المنشورات والكتب التي نشرت على مدى سنوات عديده في اليمن اتضح للكاتب ابرهارد لوتز بعض النقاط والمفاهيم الهامه ومنها أن سيطرة الشيوخ ذو الوجاهه والمكانت الرفيعه أفسد خطط التقدم والتطوير لاعضاء الهيئات التعاونية المحليه الذين حاولوا جاهدين ابقاء هذه الهيئات خالية من هذه العناصر التقليديه ولكن في نفس الوقت كانت هذه العناصر تنال الكثير من الاحترام والقبول من قبل الناس الذين ليس لديهم أي معارضة في تنصيب هذه العناصر كرؤساء للهيئات التعاونية المحلية. ولقد سرد لاكاتب لوتز بعض التحليلات الواضحة مثل أن المقدم ابراهيم محمد الحمدي (رئيس اليمن من عام ١٩٧٤م حتى ١٩٧٧م) حاول استخدام الحركات التعاونيه لترسيخ دعايم حكمه باهمال وعزل التكوينات القبليه التقليديه والتي نهاية الامر أدت الى الاحاطه بحكمه. ويؤكد الكاتب لوتز على اهمية الانتخابات الاولية العامه لمجالس الهيئات التعاونية المحليه والتي أقيمت في عام ١٩٧٥م ولاول مره في تاريخ اليمن محل فيات الشعب تدلي بأصواتها وليس فقط طبقات محدودة من المجتمع اليمني.

اما الفصل الثالث (فريتز بيبنبورج، الحركة التعاودنة اليمنية وسيرها بعد عام ١٩٨٥م) فيعطي لمحة شامله للتطور في الحركات التعاونيه اليمنيه بعد الندوة التي عقدت في صنعاء عام ١٩٨٥م وانشار الى أن الحركات التعاونيه اليمنيه خضعت لعملية ازدياد في سيطرة ونفوذ الحكومه مما ادى الى تأثير ذات وجهين متضادين. ان الاشراف الفني وتنسيق النشاطات المختلفه لما يسمى حالياً بالمجالس المحليه للتطوير التعاوني تعتبر من التغييرات الايجابيه. وعلاوة على ذلك فشكل تنظيم المجالس المحليه للتطوير التعاوني وفقاً لاحدث النظم الديمقراطيه والمدعومه بأنتخابات شامله لأول مره في تاريخ اليمن سابقة هامة لإنتخابات مجلس الشورى (الترلمان) والتي عقدت في ٥ يوليو ١٩٨٨م. هذا من ناحية ومن ناحية اخرى ادى التدخل السياسي المتصاعد من قبل الحكومه في الشئون الداخليه وتكوينات المجالس المحليه الى انخفاض الحماس والمثابره التي كانت موجوده من قبل أعضاء هذه المجالس واصبحت المبادرات والتنظيمات والتمويل لا يأتي من الناس المهتمين مباشرةً بل ظلت تحت مسؤولية بعض الموظفين المدنيين والاداريين الذين تدفع

اضفى على التلقائيه في العمل التعاوني عوامل جديده جعلت دورها يتعاظم ويزداد فعاليه.

وهذا الكتيب هو محاولة لابراز اهمية التنمية الاقليمية والتوزيع العادل لثمار التنميه بأعتبار ان عدالة توزيع الدخل يعد هدفاً محورياً من اهداف التنميه. كما يتعرض هذا الكتيب لابرز مقررات التنمية الاقليمية، والاثر الحيوي البالغ للعمل التعاوني كأسلوب عملي للتنمية، أثبت قدراته الفائقه على ايصال ثمار التنميه الى كل سهل وجبل داخل الدوله. وهو بذلك يحد من ظاهره جيوب الفقر التي تعاني منها العديد من بلدان العالم الثالث.

كتابنا هذا يتكون من ستة فصول .. ثلاثة منها كانت اصلاً قد قدمت كأوراق عمل الى ندوة أقيمت في صنعاء خلال الفترة 13- 14 مايو سنة 1985م بالتعاون بين كل من جمعية الاقتصاديين اليمنيين واكاديمية الاساتذه من اجل السلام العالمي (Professors World Peace Academy - Middle East Division). وقد اقيمت هذه الندوة تحت عنوان «الحركات التعاونية ــ تجربة عالمية (Coperative Movements – A World Experience) وقد حظيت الندوه باهتمام العديد من المسئولين المختصين في الحكومة، ومن قبل ممثلين عن السلك الدبلوماسي الذين حضروا الندوة.

وقد رأينا اضافة بقية الفصول من اجل اكتمال الغرض من هذا المؤلف الذي يهدف الى تبيان الاهمية البالغة للتنمية الاقليمية، والدور الحيوي للحركة التعاونية في الدفع بالتنمية الاقليمية ورفع مستوى الاقاليم الاقل نمواً فضلاً عن دورها في عملية التنمية بشكل عام.

في الفصل الاول (ضرار عبدالدائم ، الحركه التعاونيه في اليمنية، البداية والتطور) يشير الباحث الى الاصول الشعبيه للتعاونيات في اليمن. ولقد أوضح بأن الناس بدأوا من الصفر وحافزهم الاساسي اتى من رضاهم وحماسهم لتحسين ظروف معيشتهم وكانت المساهمات مقصوره على المعونات او الهبات المالية والتي ضحي المواطنون من اجل الحصول عليها وتوفيرها للناس. ويوضح الاخ ضرار وباسهاب وبطريقة عملية او طريقة أنشاء اتحاد الهيئات التعاونية اليمنية والمجلس الخاص بالثلاث المؤتمرات الاولى. لقد كان الهدف الرئيسي من انشاء اتحاد الهيئات التعاونية هو مساعدة وخدمة الهيئات التعاونية المحليه بواسطة توجيه الاعتمادات الماليه والخبرات وقد نالت هذه التجربة الكثير من الاهتمام والمتابعه من المؤسسات النظيره لها في بعض الدول في جميع انحاء العالم. ولقد أشاد الجميع وهتفوا بالتصفيق الحار لهذه التجربة الفريده من نوعها في المؤتمرات التي حضرها اتحاد الهيئات التعاونية. أن الانجازات التي حققتها الهيئات التعاونية المحليه قبل اقامة

مقدمة

امكانات المجتمع. وبدون المشاركة الشعبيه الفاعله واقحام المجتمع في هذه العمليه بكل فئاته وامكاناته بدون ذلك لن يكتب لها النجاح. ولو نظرنا الى الموضوع من نافذة علم السياسه وعلم الاجتماع لوصلنا الى ذات النتيجه التي تقتضي العمل على عدالة التوزيع بين الاقاليم المختلفه وشمولية التنمية. وعند الحديث عن التحضر (من الحضاره) فإن اسلوب التنمية وشموليتها ايضاً يلعب دوراً مميزاً.

حيث ان التنمية عبر التعاون والمشاركة الشعبيه الفعاله هو المقصود فعلاً وبدونه لايمكن الاستدلال على تكون ارضيه حضاريه تكفل الرقي والازدهار الى مراتب حضاريه اعلى. فالحضاره تقاس بمدى التحسن المعنوي والمادي في حياة الناس كل الناس، وهي ثمرة جهودهم جميعاً. والعمل التعاوني كان ولايزال اسلوباً راقياً للعمل الجماعي عرفته البشريه منذ اقدم العصور.

اذ انه على مر التاريخ وفي ظل كل الانظمه التي عرفها الانسان من المشاعيه والجماعات البدائيه الى الاقطاع والنظم القبليه، فالراسماليه والاشتراكيه ومع ظهور الدوله بوظائفها المختلفه والتي تمتد من التطرف في المركزيه الى التطرف في اللامركزيه. في ظل كل هذه الانظمه ظلت البشريه تمارس العمل التعاوني بأشكال مختلفه تفرضها طبيعة الحياه بما فيها من تحديات وصعاب.

ولقد تطور العمل التعاوني سواء في الجانب التنظيمي او في نطاق المهام الموكله اليه. حيث بات يغطي مساحة كبيره من الانشطه الخدميه والانتاجيه والاستهلاكيه، فضلاً عما يمثله من ضمان فعال في مواجهة الكوارث والنكبات. وفي البلدان الناميه تزداد اهمية العمل التعاوني لا لكونه رديف فاعل للقطاعات الاخرى في عملية التنمية فحسب بل لما يمثله من مقدره على حشد الطاقات، واقحام كل افراد الشعب في خضم التنميه وفي توزيع ثمارها على مختلف الاقاليم. ففي مثل هذه البلدان عادة ما تكون الموارد المتاحه للحكومه متواضعه لدرجة يصعب عليها تنفيذ كافة المشاريع الضروريه لاستمرار زخم التنميه وهو ما يؤدي الى تركز جهود التنمية في بعض المدن الرئيسيه المحظوظه ومن هنا يأتي دور التعاونيات.

ولليمن تاريخ عريق في مجال ممارسة العمل التعاوني يمتد الى حقب مغرقه في القدم حيث شكل التعاون احد ابرز القيم النبيله التي يرتكز عليها المجتمع اليمني ويعتمد عليها في مواجهة التخلف. وقد كان لعوامل عده مرتبطه بالارض والانسان، كان لهذه العوامل دورها البارز في استمرار وتطور هذا الاسلوب من العمل الجماعي البالغ الرقي.

ومع بزوغ فجر ثورة ٢٦ من سبتمبر و ١٤ اكتوبر توسعت آفاق التعاون حيث بدأت حقبة جديده من العمل التعاوني وتميزت بنوع من التنظيم والتقنيه والدعم الحكومي الذي

على مستوى الاستيراد الذي صار مألوفاً. اذ انه مع استمرار هذا الاتجاه تتزايد احتياجات البلد النامي الى المزيد من الموارد التي تهدرها لا لزيادة حجم الاستيراد بل حتى للمحافظة على مستواه المألوف فحسب. حين تصل دولة ناميه الى مرحلة كهذه تصبح الحكومة مضطره تحت وطأة ضغوط القلة المترفه المستفيده لتوجيه كل الجهود التي يطلق عليها تعبير « جهود تنمويه » (رغم انها لاتمت الى التنميه في شيء) توجه هذه الجهود الى عملية المحافظه على مستوى الاستيراد. وبالتالي يصبح الهم الاول للحكومه هو الحصول على النقد الاجنبي للمحافظه على سير الاستيراد الذي قد يجرف البلاد ولكنه يحافظ على الحكومه ولو مؤقتاً.

وفي سعي البلاد النامي لفك خيوط العنكبوت والفلات من هذا الشرك اللعين يتلفت في كل جانب بحثاً عن مصدر للنقد الاجنبي فيقترض اكثر ويصدر اكثر من المواد الخام والمنتجات الزراعيه التي تكون الاسواق المحلية أحوج ماتكون اليها لإطعام الفقراء وايجاد عمل مناسب لهم. وتدريجياً تجد البلاد الناميه نفسها في نفق مظلم وتزداد فيه أعباء الديون وخدمة الديون ويزداد فيه الفقر والعوز والغنى الفاحش في آن واحد، فتستمر باطراد عملية اخذ اللقمه من فم الفقير الى فم الغني.

لايقف الامر عند هذا الحد بالطبع ففي ظل هذا الاسلوب الشائع للتحديث يمكن الاشاره الى جملة من السلبيات المرفقه. تذكر منها على سبيل المثال :- تزايد الهجرة من الريف الى المدن فتكتض المدن بالسكان وتحاط بما يسمى بأحزمة الفقر العاطله عن العمل فينتشر البؤس ومعه كافة الاوبئه وينتشر الفساد الخلقي بأشكال جديده غير معهودة ومنظمه وتزداد الجرائم المنظمه من كافة الانواع وتزداد الافواه التي تطلب الرغيف.

وبالمقابل يفقد الريف الجزء المنتج من القوة العامله فيقل الانتاج الزراعي ويزداد الميول للاستهلاك فتتزايد وطأة الفقر والعوز ومعه الشعور بالحرمان والتطلع الى المدينه المحظوظة في محاولة للخلاص من واقع البؤس في الريف الى واقع اكثر بؤساً في حزام الفقر في المدينه.

هذا الواقع المؤلم من الممكن تداركه باتباع سياسات تنمويه مناسبه، فبالامكان مضاعفه أثر الاستثمارات بمجرد العمل على توزيعها بشكل اقتصادي عادل على مختلف الاقاليم. فتوسيع نطاق الاستثمار ليمتد الى الريف الذي يقطنه اغلب السكان يؤدي الى ارتفاع مستوى الانتاجيه وبالتالي ارتفاع مستوى الدخل الحقيقي وهو امر يؤدي الى زيادة الطلب على السلع والخدمات المنتجة محلياً مما يزيد الحافز للاستثمار و الخ٢ .

كما ان عملية التنمية والتقدم صارت تتطلب جهوداً مضنيه ومتواصله وتتطلب تعبئة كل

الاستثمار وبالتالي انخفاض مستوى الانتاجيه هذا من جانب العرُض. وفي جانب الطلب يؤدي المستوى المتدني للانتاجيه الى انخفاض مستوى الدخل الحقيقي وهذا بدوره يؤدي الى انخفاض الطلب على السلع والخدمات وهو أمر يجعل الحافز للاستثمار يتضاءل، ويتضائل معه مقدار رؤوس الاموال المستخدمه في الانتاج، ويترتب على هذا الاخير انخفاض مستوى الانتاجيه للعامل.

فبامكان أي من البلدان الناميه كسر هذه الحلقه اللعينه والفلات من آسارها باتباع الاسلوب المناسب للتنميه. وعلى سبيل المثال بإمكاننا زيادة الحافز للاستثمار باستخدام سياسات تؤدي الى تزايد الطلب.

فمشكلة البلدان الناميه ان جهود التنميه في كثير منها تنصب في عاصمة الدولة وقلة من المدن الاخرى او في إقليم معين. وهذا أمر يؤدي الى تخمه اقتصاديه اذا جازلنا التعبير في مدينه او إقليم معين بل عند فئه قليلة من سكان ذلك الاقليم دون غيرهم، مبقيا على بقية اجزاء البلاد دون تقدم يذكر. هذه الحاله الشاذه تفرز جملة من العوائق في سبيل التنميه. من هذه العوائق انها تؤدي الى تفاقم الطلب على السلع الكماليه المسترده الذي يحصل نتاج تزايد الدخل لدى القله المترفه في المدن او الاقليم المحظوظ. يحصل ذلك بينما يظل مستوى الطلب لدى الغالبيه العظمى من السكان دون تغيير يذكر. هذه الحقيقه يترتب عليها تركز الاستثمارات لرؤوس الاموال في قطاع التجاره الخارجيه (الاستيراد المربح) عوضاً عن ان تصب في قطاعات انتاجيه تلبي احتياجات القطاعات العريضه من السكان وفي نفس الوقت تعمل كمحرك لعملية التنميه. ومع استمرار هذه العمليه التي يمكن تسميتها بالتحديث الجزئي او بتنمية التخلف او تشويه عملية التنميه كلما استمرت هذه العمليه أغرت المزيد من رؤوس الاموال الى الانتقال الى قطاع التجاره الخارجيه زادت وبالتالي من امكانات إفقار البلاد. لماذا؟ تصب المساعدات والقروض ودخل الحكومه الممول من الضرائب والجمارك، وغيرها في إقليم معين فتتحول هذه الامكانات الى سيل جارف من الطلب على السلع الكماليه التي يتعذر الحصول عليها محلياً فتستورد بطبيعة الحال من الخارج. ومع الزمن تتفاقم القدرات الاستهلاكيه ويتفاقم معها مستوى الاستيراد ومع هذا الاخير يتزايد الطلب على النقد الاجنبي فتتعالى قيمته بالنسبه للعمله المحليه التي تشرع بإنحدار والتضائل أمام العملات الاجنبيه.

تزايد سعر الصرف لصالح النقد الاجنبي يؤدي نتيجة ذات وجهين : -
فمن جهه يؤدي الى إنحدار سريع لاسعار السلع والخدمات المحليه مقيمه بالنقد الاجنبي، ومن جهة أخرى يؤدي الى انخفاض القدره على الاستيراد بل وصعوبة المحافظة

بسم الله الرحمن الرحيم

مقدمة

بقلم الدكتور محمد احمد السعيدي

ان زيادة الدخل لفئة معينه او لطبقه او حتى لاقليم معين لا يعتبر بأي حال تنميه. فعملية التنميه بشكل مبسط انما تتمثل في التصدي لعقبات التنمية الاقتصاديه.

هذه العقبات تشتد وطئتها في كون كل منها تشكل سبب ونتيجه لغيرها من العقبات في آن واحد. وهي بهذه الصفه تشكل مايسمى بالحلقات المفرغة للفقر ١ والحقيقة كما تبدو لي ان الجزء الاكبر من المشكله التي ترتكز عليها نظرية كهذه انما ترجع الى السبل المستخدمه في عملية التنمية اكثر من كونها ترجع الى خصائص معينة تميز المجتمعات الناميه. فهي اذاً ليست صفة ملازمه او مرتبطه بالمجتمعات الناميه دون غيرها يستحيل الفكاك من آسارها بقدر ارتباطها بالنهج الذي تسير عليه اي تجربة تنموية ، بدليل ان هناك بلدان ناميه استطاعت الفكاك من آسار الحلقات المفرغة هذه.

فانخفاض الدخل الحقيقي في البلدان الناميه الذي يعد نتيجة لإنخفاض مستوى الانتاجيه يترتب عليه ضآلة المقدرة على الادخار وهذا بدوره يؤدي الى انخفاض مستوى

الحركة التعاونية في اليمن وقضية التنمية الإقليمية

الدكتور محمد احمد السعيدي

اكاديمية الاساتذة من اجل السلام

Bei Fragen zur Produktsicherheit wenden Sie sich bitte an:
If you have any questions regarding product safety,
please contact:

Walter de Gruyter GmbH
Genthiner Straße 13
10785 Berlin
productsafety@degruyterbrill.com